THE TWITTER WHO SERIES

A NEW WHOVIAN'S JOURNEY THROUGH CLASSIC TERRITORY 140 CHARACTERS AT A TIME

VOLUME 1: THE FIRST DOCTOR
VOLUME 2: THE SECOND DOCTOR

UPCOMING:

VOLUME 3: THE THIRD DOCTOR

D1739167

TWITTER WHO VOLUME 2: THE SECOND DOCTOR

RAGGEDY MOON BOOKS

TWITTER WHO VOLUME 2: THE SECOND DOCTOR

2014
Raggedy Moon Books

Cover design by Hannah J. Rothman
hannahjrothman.com

Book interior design by Faith L. Justice
faithljustice.com

ISBN: 0692026193
ISBN-13: 978-0692026199
Epub ISBN: 978-1311971227

Previously Published:
"The Macra Terror" Copyright © 2012 Hannah J. Rothman, first
appeared in *Outside In*, Robert Smith?, ed., ATB Publishing, 2012

Raggedy Moon Books
Brooklyn, NY, USA
raggedymoonbooks.com

CONTENTS

Introduction
Season 4
With Ben and Polly

With Ben, Polly, and Jamie
With Jamie and Victoria
Season 5
With Jamie and Zoe
Season 6
Bonus

ACKNOWLEDGEMENTS

Special thanks to Stephen Fry, for whom I got on Twitter in the first place; Toria, whose live-Tweeting of "The End of Time, Part 2" made me want to give it a shot as well; Dave, who actually got me watching the show and graciously supplied the DVDs of seasons 1-4 for our weekly marathons; all my Whovian friends on Tumblr, especially the loving and supportive circle of the TPC with whom I became active in fandom like never before; Mom, who pointed to my blog and reminded me that I had quite a bit of material there that I could do something with.

"There are some corners of the universe which have bred the most terrible things, things which act against everything that we believe in. They must be fought!"

-The Second Doctor

Twitter Who Volume 2: The Second Doctor

Hannah J. Rothman

INTRODUCTION

Here's where things get interactive.

In my sophomore year of college, a little less than a year after I began this project, one of my lovely followers at the blog hub on LiveJournal joined a certain little website called Tumblr. A few weeks later, I caved and joined Tumblr myself. It was the best and worst Internet-related decision I'd made in a while. On the downside, I spent a preposterous amount of time on Tumblr and it quickly overrode TV Tropes as the website that tied me down and glued me to the computer late into the night. On the plus-side, I now had a new and unique venue to participate in Doctor Who fandom. In particular, it became my preview peanut gallery for the entire Patrick Troughton era. Which brings me to the Terrible People Club.

I made quite a few friends through the Classic Who fandom on Tumblr, and a good number of them were particular fans of Two and Jamie. One in particular would regularly post pictures of the two of them in wacky photomanips (such as ads for Jamie-brand moisturizer called Highland Fresh) with the caption "I am a terrible person," or some variant. Eventually it caught on as Our Thing and we collectively put out reams of Two-and-Jamie-adoration and lovingly called ourselves Terrible for it. We made fan art, posted pictures with silly captions, and had one rather eventful night of round-robin fanfiction writing that rendered us unable to look at roast beef sandwiches the same way ever again. I'd been an active participant in several online fandoms before, but in most of them I'd felt like the baby of the group. I was the one most likely to accidentally post something offensive, write un-ironically bad fanfic, or be the resident Annoying Thirteen-Year-Old. But with the Who fandom on Tumblr, especially with the Terrible People Club, I felt that I was amongst peers. Most of us were around the same age and the same points in our lives, so we were able to connect on more levels than just our common fandom. I've even had the pleasure of meeting some of them in person, and will likely be meeting more of them in the future. Speaking of meeting in person…

The Second Doctor holds a special place for me offline since, as of this writing, it's the only era of the show for which I've met all the living companion actors. I know it's good form for fans to keep a mental barrier between an actor and the characters they play, but I had good experiences with all four of them and anecdotes from conventions are likely to work their way into the character retrospectives in this volume. Yeah, I know the old adage goes "never meet your heroes," but if your heroes are actors from Doctor Who, it's an adage you can safely ignore.

THE POWER OF THE DALEKS

Written by David Whitaker and Dennis Spooner
Aired: November 5 – December 10, 1966

I'm going to have to get used to seeing Hartnell's opening but not subsequently seeing Hartnell for a few serials.

"His face, his head, look at it!" Aaaaaaaaaaaand HELLO PAT!

FOOTAGE!
"'This old body of mine is wearing a bit thin'..."
"So he just gets a NEW one?"

You can hear it Patrick...the drums...when will it stop?

I'll bet that's what the old BBC sheet meant about regeneration having the effect of a bad acid trip.

Actual footage of Two moving! "...It's over..." (and he's got his creepy face on. Or maybe it's just the lighting.)

I'm delightfully impressed with how frequently this episode has random clips of surviving footage.

And there goes One's ring. But wait, how does he already have the Lucky Charms Marshmallow Suspenders on?

"It's not just his face that's changed, he doesn't even act like him!" But you haven't even seen him DO that much yet.

"The Doctor kept a diary, didn't he?" AHA! So THIS is where the 500 year diary comes in...

OH WAIT THERE'S THE RECORDER! And I feel like I should recognize this tune.

Wow. Ben most certainly does not approve of Two. Don't worry, you'll have almost a whole season to get used to him.

Hello there, Two's Giant Hat!

Crap, I've got Two's tune (twone?) stuck in my head now.

"So you've come at last. I'm from Earth. I'm the Examine-" *BANG* ...wow. That was one of the fastest deaths I've seen on this show.

Oh, hello unexpected!bum-shot.

I'm impressed that Polly finds beauty in this alien mercury swamp of death.

Aaaaaaand now she's getting ill. #thingsthatshouldntsurprisemeatall

Well, at least they were rescued by locals pretty quickly.

Is Two just hitting sour notes, or does he just aim for really high pitches to intermittently shut Ben up?

"What is your brief?"
"I am the Examiner."
"Why are you here?"
"...To examine."

So Two's pretending to be the dead guy while trying to solve the mystery of his murder. Crafty crafty Doctor.

Looks like they've about got that mysterious capsule opened...

Ah yes, those are definitely Dalek-shaped doorways.

Waaaaaaaait why does that one telesnap look like Polly isn't wearing pants.

looks at bigger version Oh. She's wearing tight shorts, that's why.

"Polly, Ben, come in and meet the Daleks." And said so CALMLY too.

Wait, was that a live Dalek mutant scuttling across the floor?

PAT. YOUR FACE. I LOVE YOUR FACE.

FOOTAGE "IS ALL THAT IS NEEDED TO WIPE OUT THIS ENTIRE COLONY!"

"Lesterson listen Lesterson listen Lesterson listen Lesterson listen Lesterson listen Lesterson listen Lesterson listen Lesterson listen..."

Ah, this must be the first big never-underestimate-Two moment.

Lesterson shall revive the Daleks...FOR SCIENCE!

Apparently Two just almost ate a hidden microphone. In a piece of fruit. What will they think of next?

Considering where that Dalek's sucker-arm is, I'd almost say it was trying to cop a feel.

Ooo, we even get Dalek-eye vision!

Scientists surrounding a Dalek and running experiments on it...this reminds me distinctly of the episode Dalek.

Sir, you have been DALEK'D. You're very very very lucky to be alive.

Oh wait, the BBC is telling me otherwise.

Polly, I really don't believe what you say about how you can tell some people are good "just by looking at them."

On the other hand, the characters keep saying that the guy ISN'T dead. MAKE UP YOUR MINDS, PEOPLE.

Footage! The Doctor through Dalek-vision!

"I. AM. YOUR. SER-VANT." But I thought tame!Daleks didn't happen until Evil of the Daleks. Although, they were in Victory of the Daleks too.

So the Dalek is conveniently forgetting to be evil and no one will listen to Two. I predict that those who survive will regret it later.

"The Daleks are the important thing."
"AH! Congratulations Ben!"
"Whadid I do whadid I DO?"
"You just used your brains that's what you did!"

For some reason, I always find myself bugged by subplots in Troughton serials that just focus on the local characters. Show me more Two!

Sorry Ben, but I don't think your plan to steal people and hide them would go over very well.

And now the BBC presents, Chemistry: by A Dalek.

So now I'm going to be That Terrible Person who points out that the removal of a Dalek's gun could be symbolic of castration.

And now it's official: Resno IS actually in fact really dead.

"Can I leave it to you? I'm going to go back to the restroom."
"But..."
"Somebody's got to clear it up!"
#dodgyimplicationsinsomecountries

So last time Polly was told by the locals to just Stay In The Kitchen, but now she's actually being CHLOROFORMED. Really, guys? Really?

Two seems more concerned with his recorder and the Dalek than with the mysterious fate of Polly. I mean, priorities, but still...

"But she is MISSING!"
"Oh no no no no."

"Oh yes yes yes yes!"
"Oh no no no."

I think that's the first time I've heard a Dalek stop itself in mid-sentence to correct itself.

Ah, hello there, small Dalek army.

"When I say 'run,' run like a rabbit...RUN!"

Something in my brain went "random note" when that paper was slipped under the door. Amazingly, it was right.

"I would like a hat like that." Oh come on, Two, what's wrong with the hat you have now? It makes you look taller!

"DO. I. BRING. LI-QUID. FOR. YOUR. VI-SI-TORS?" ...... depends which liquid you're referring to.

Ah, they seem to still have the Daleks-move-around-by-conduction-in-the-floor thing in effect. Wonder how long that'll last...

NO, DALEKS, STOP IT. WE DON'T WANT TO DRINK YOUR LIQUID.

Congratulations, Two and Ben, you can do maths!

So FINALLY after all this time, Lesterson gets that maybe the Cosmic Hobo is onto something with this "HOLY SHIT DALEKS ARE EVIL D:" thing.

LESTERSON, EVERYTHING YOU KNOW IS A LIE. THE DALEKS ARE EVIL, YOUR FRIEND IS DEAD, AND SANTA CLAUS DOES NOT EXIST.

"There's only one explanation: the Daleks are reproducing themselves." Which makes me wonder how a Dalek version of The Talk would go.

"MO-THER. WHERE. DO. BA-BIES. COME. FROM?"
"WELL. SON. WHEN. DAV-ROS. AND. SCI-ENCE. LOVE. EACH. OTHER. VERY. MUCH..."

5

Aww, I would say that Janley and Lesterson made a cute couple if she wasn't a slightly psychotic manipulative bitch.

If the coded messages are simple anagrams, I'm surprised no one picked up on it before.

Ah, Doctor-in-a-cage. As is to be expected.

I could've sword I heard dogs barking just now...

Footage! It's Daleks on an assembly line! #everyoneisfucked

I think Lesterson just reached his Sanity Event Horizon.

I have to admit, with all the black-and-white contrast the close-ups on the Daleks' eyestalks are actually quite chilling.

Ah, there's Polly again! We didn't see any of you last episode, did we?

sigh Nobody even listens to the madman.

"You think you're very tough, don't you? Pushing girls around. I'd like to see you come up against a real man."
"Like who?"
"Like Ben."

Ben Jackson is a real man. A real man. #arealman

So of course the real governor comes back and within about 5 minutes, he's dead.

"WHY. DO. HU-MAN. BE-INGS. KILL. HU-MAN. BE-INGS?" That might be one of the most startlingly profound things a Dalek has ever said ever.

Aw crapmonkeys, there's a fight scene going on and I can only half-follow it.

Well, at least now Two and Polly are back together.

Wait, so HOW long have the Daleks just been standing there yelling "EX-TER-MIN-ATE" over and over again?

And now we have FOOTAGE to accompany this endless cacophony!

Ben and Polly back together at last!

Hide yo' Bens, hide yo' Pollys, an' hide yo' Doctahs, 'cause they exterminatin' errebody out here.

"BUT. WE. ARE. YOUR. FRIENDS."
"WE. WILL. SERVE. YOU!"

This is gonna sound completely insane, but the way the shadows are arranged it almost looks like there's a giant bald eagle in the doorway.

Okay, it doesn't look quite that way in the high-res telesnap, but...agh. #myimaginationistoovivid

Guys, Lesterson's creeper-face is truly creeperific. I mean WOW. Have fun sleeping tonight, kids. #imreallyverysorry

Awww, I think Velmar was in love with Janley. Shame she was kind of a bitch.

The music here would probably be a lot less creepy if it didn't loop for EVERY camera change. Dead people are dead.

So it looks like Bragen's going to be the last to realize that the Daleks are DALEKS. YOU CAN'T PUT LEASHES ON DALEKS.

Wow. Lesterson's not only completely flipped, but I think he thinks he IS Dalek now.

"But you wouldn't kill me...I gave you LIFE!"
"YES. YOU. GAVE. US. LIFE." *exterminates*

And Dalek heads go S'PLODY!

YAY little bit 'o footage so we can actually see some of it!

And the moral of the story is: all corrupt leaders deserve to be shot and you can always save the day by blowing shit up.

"What'd I do? What'd I do?"

7

"You destroyed the Daleks, that's what you did!"
"Yes, I did that..."

So the locals seem to think that Two and company have caused as much damage as they prevented. Priorities, people, PRIORITIES.

Colony in shambles, countless people dead, and nobody even bothers to thank the heroes. That's a remarkably dark start to the Troughton era.

I really wish this was a surviving serial. I think the only thing keeping me from liking the locals more was that I could barely see them.

But on the plus-side, I won't have to deal with another fully-missing 6-part serial until Fury From the Deep!

Originally Posted December 19th, 2010

THE HIGHLANDERS

Written by Elwyn Jones and Gerry Davis
Aired: December 17, 1966 – January 7, 1967

And we open on the fields of Culloden, where a certain kilted young laddie is about to pipe (or cling) his way into our hearts.

Ah, hello footage of redcoats being stabbed!

BAGPIPES! It's like I'm back at Wooster... (oh well, I'll be hearing plenty more of it when Winter Break ends)

Aww, I love how Polly wants to chase after Ben because she knows he'll get in trouble if she doesn't stop him first.

"Every droplet left..." Ladies and gentlemen and fangirls, James Robert M.F. McCrimmon.

I think he just played a couple notes, too, but they seemed a bit... strangled, somehow.

Wait, what's a tam-o'-shanter...oh. THAT hat. "I would like a hat like this!" (ALSO PAT YOUR FACE)

Two, meet your future space husband.

Ben, somehow I don't think threatening them with a gun is really going to do much good.

wOh. I guess it is. Never mind...

"Will you both give us your word that you will not molest us?" #nocomment

And Alexander goes down. Ouch. But Two what is your voice.

"Doctor von Werr."
"Doctor who?"
"That's what I said."

Oh, I see, that's a GERMAN accent. And Hanover. Yes...

Wow, the redcoats are kind of assholes, aren't they?

...and they're actually considering carting some of them off as slave labor to the West Indies. What.

Is this where things begin to turn into, as they put it, The Polly Wright Show?

Oh joy, we actually get footage of them getting noosed up.

They day is saved by Grey! AKA, that guy who wants to sell the prisoners off. Yay...?

It seems to me that all highlanders are human clingwrap by nature, or something of the sort.

Bechdel Test: Passed (I think).

Polly: friends over jewelry any day. Atta girl.

"Well you bend down and I'll climb on top of you..." Come on, Hannah, give the people some context. #piggyback

Two seems to be enjoying himself in that jail cell, doesn't he?

Nice. Two caught on to the whole superstitious-Scot thing and is using astrology to tell them off.

"He's probably never heard of germs."
"What was that word?"
"It's a secret word."

Wow. The prison guards disapprove of Two's recorder playing even more than Ben.

Has anyone else noticed that Jamie's kind of adorable when he's mad? #ofcourseyouhave

Ladies and gentlemen, The Polly Wright Show: in which Polly is awesome.

I'm still trying to work out exactly what Two has up his sleeves (other than Prince Charles' silk standard, and that was in his waistcoat).

Oh. Actually, that's exactly what Two had up his sleeve. And now he's threatening to accidentally shoot Grey in the face o___O

"Do you suffer from headaches?"
"No I don't!"
SLAM "No headaches?"
Thank you, Two, for reminding us of those times when violence is funny.

This should be a children's nursery rhyme: Doctor Two is greater than you. (Or algebra: Two > you.)

Poor Ffinch, his men are really keen on delaying his rescue from the pit, aren't they?

Uh oh, Two's hiding in a scullery and there's a mean ol' nasty redcoat coming! WHAT WILL HE DO? Is there a disguise? THERE IS!

So guess where the boys are now? #ONABOAT

OH MY GOD LADY!TWO WHAT IS YOUR VOICE EVEN.

I just realized: the slave trader's name is "Trask." Sounds more like a name used in one of the sci-fi Who stories, not a historical.

WHICH REMINDS ME. This is the last alien-free historical Who story until Black Orchid, isn't it? I wonder if I'll miss them...

"...and Jamie, son of Donald McCrimmon, a piper like his father and his father's father." #jamesrobertMFmccrimmon

Ah, and Ben finally catches on! Next question is, can he come up with an escape plan?

("Polly practices stabbing with Kirsty's dirk, however, she drops it.") Is Polly gonna hafta stab a bitch?

So I see Polly and Kirsty with those oranges and all I can think of is the Orange Girls mishap from one of PG Wodehouse's Jeeves stories. (The mishap in question being that girls in a play are supposed to have orange balls of yarn to throw at the audience but get real oranges.)

And now I'm going to go a step further and quote Monty Python: "But this is a temperate zone!"

Apparently someone just called the Doctor a wench. I didn't realize until now how much I needed that in my life.

Wow. Polly and Kirsty are having so much fun abusing Ffinch, aren't they?

Ah, so they're not really being carted off as slaves, but as indentured servants. Or maybe I have that wrong.

One of the preferred ways of defying The Man in the Whoniverse seems to be tearing up paper, doesn't it?

An alien time traveler dressed as an old woman is threatening a clerk with a gun into playing a game of cards. This show.

"We ladies are going to leave first..." Note that Two's using his regular voice to tell him this.

Polly basically just told Two that he's a pretty girl. #patricktroughtonisaprettygirl

12

Two, I really don't like this attitude you've suddenly adopted, but you're such a pretty girl.

Also, WHY are you so gun-happy in this story? I really don't even. "You must've robbed the Duke's arsenal!" "Yes...something like that."

And the ring comes into play again! Also, I know I've been saying it a lot lately but...Pat. Your face.

Wait Ben just got thrown over the side of the boat what HEY IT'S THAT OTHER THEME TUNE VARIATION I REALLY LIKE.

Ah, of course. Ben is an Able Seaman, after all, and was probably trained in tying and untying ship-knots.

Oh wait, THIS must be the awesome escape my Blog watchers were talking about...

Gee, that redcoat with the bandaged head and the fake mustache and PAT YOUR FACE sure looks familiar, doesn't he?

Wow, looks like Grey really does have some small sense of justice if he's going out of his way to haul the highlanders off legally.

And Ben actually gets to explain his stunt! Turns out it had nothing to do with untying knots and everything to do with flexing his muscles.

To reiterate the point: Patrick Troughton was a very pretty girl.

Yes, Two, you would like a hat like EVERY hat.

And I'm curious: how exactly is it that you already know that Jamie has "soft hands and face?"

"CREAG AN TUIRE!!!" Because NOBODY tries to touch Jamie and gets away with it (except the Doctor).

(Of course, with them it's a mutual thing. A thing called The Cling.)

Ooo yay! Censored in Australia...I mean, surviving fight scene footage!

Jamie just threw Trask overboard. #jamesrobertMFmccrimmon #BAMFladdiesinkilts

"We never even said goodbye to Jamie."
"No, he just disappeared. I wonder where he went to?"
"Right here!" *completely expected Jamie*

Aww, poor Ffinch is going to be Team Two's substitute hostage, isn't he?

Well, not really hostage, but close. At least Polly gave him his ID back.

And he gets to set Grey on the road to what's coming to 'im, and he even gets a goodbye kiss from Polly. Aww.

"Doctor, can we take him with us?"
"If he teaches me to play the bagpipes."
"If you want, Doctor!"

Welcome aboard the TARDIS, Jamie! I'm sure we'll be seeing a lot more of you over the course of the next few seasons.

Originally Posted December 24th, 2010

14

THE UNDERWATER MENACE

Written by Geoffrey Orme
Aired: January 14 – February 4, 1967

"Unresistingly, Jamie allows himself to be drawn inside the TARDIS." #thingsthatsoundalotdirtierthantheyreallyare

I think I just found out where all of Jeeves' "as the poet Burns says" lines came from.

"Please let it be Chelsea 1966..."
"I hope it's the Daleks, I DON'T think..."
"Prehistoric monsters... :D"
"What have I come upon?"

Jamie, trust me, you're going to be coming upon a new thing every few weeks for the next several years or so.

Also, I think this is one of the only times when the TARDIS crew has wished for individual destinations before they land.

Oh, hello Unexpected Color Shot!

Extinct volcano. Logical conclusion: climb up it! (and now Team Two is just "Polly and her friends?")

"As she bends to pick it up, a shadow falls over her." Ooo, nice contrast effect!

Oh wow, they're actually addressing the issues of rapid descent and nitrogen compression. Why wasn't this in The Hungry Earth/Cold Blood?

Or maybe it was and I just forgot. I haven't seen those since they aired.

Oh. Um, hello Unexpected Troughton Crotch Shot.

"Cavemen? Hey Jamie, you better watch it. With that kilt, someone might mistake you for a bird!" ...what?

I'm not sure if he means "bird" as slang for "girl" or an actual bird. I'm assuming it's the former.

Ohhhh, THAT'S how "Mexico Olympiad" helped Ben and Polly tell the future.

Oh neat, Jamie knows Gaelic! *is made of enough language-fail to not be sure if all 18th century Scots knew English and Gaelic*

"Women and children last." Oh come on, Two, where's your sense of chivalry?

"What's got into 'im?"
"I don't know, I've never seen him go for food like this before; it's usually hats!"

A "striking figure in splendid robes"...wearing an epically bizarre hat and carrying a fish mask. #doctorwhofashions

I expect when someone "regrets to say" that you're to play an "important role" in their festival, I can only assume it means "sacrifice."

Team Two about to be dumped into shark-infested waters? I'm surprised this isn't the cliffhanger.

I'm surprised Zaroff's entrance didn't merit a musical cue. I mean, he DID just save Team Two from getting nommed by sharks.

"I could feed you to my pet octopus, yes?!"
"Yes!"
What is it with mad scientists and cephalopods?

16

Ahhhhh, those weird fish-people-things from stuff.

WAIT A SEC. ARE THEY IN ATLANTIS?

THEY ARE. (real ancient mythology in my Doctor Who? It's more likely than you'd think)

The real cliffhanger: Polly's about to go under the knife.

Attention creepers: your fish-surgery has been delayed due to Two having fun with wire cutters.

Draining the oceans to bring Atlantis back to the surface? SURE, WHY NOT?

"Just one small question: why do you want to blow up the world?" Zaroff's answer seems to be, in short, "because it would be AWESOME."

Two doesn't need to fight his way out of awkward situations, he just does science to it!

Well it looks like Two has a chance of getting the priest on his side, now that he's so conveniently voiced his distrust of Zaroff aloud.

I don't think water boils quite THAT fast, you guys.

Please hold for the ruler of Atlantis. While you wait, some light music from Patrick the Doctor and Squeaky the Recorder.

Aaaaand somehow they've lost Jamie. I wonder what he's off clinging to.

Boi what is on your head.

Oh. OH. Jamie's not just clinging, he's clinging for his LIFE. (why did I accidentally type "LOVE" first...)

(Of course, I can think of a lot of good reasons to cling to your LOVE.)

Considering how this serial was probably scripted initially, I'll bet that scene only exists for Jamie to have something happen to him.

Wait a sec, I thought the idol and the braziers were in the same room. How did Polly not wake up when the jar exploded?

Oh Two, how long has it been since I've seen you actually moving? Not since this summer, I think.

Holy crap, that comment about "have you seen his eyes" might actually have some plot significance after all.

And now that things are actually moving, I can have proper appreciation for WHAT ARE THEY EVEN WEARING.

"I AM THE VOICE OF AMDO! HEAR ME!" In other words, "I AM OZ! THE GREAT AND TERRIBLE!" Or something like it.

Ben is playing god. This is just amazing and wonderful.

Zaroff is truly a creepy lord of creepers. Seriously. So much creep.

"But slaves, like worms, can be made to turn." Umm...Two, forgive me if I don't see the connection here.

You can tell how new Jamie is to all this by his distance from Two right now.

TWO. BUT WHAT ARE YOU WEARING. WHAT IS EVERYBODY WEARING. AND WHAT IS THE MUSIC EVEN, WHILE WE'RE AT IT.

Polly almost got pitchforked through a carpet. Wow, guys. Just...wow.

Ladies and gentlemen, we have rubber-clad cling.

......oh. Oh goodness, those things really *are* tight, aren't they?

CHAOS IN THE MARKET! I'm really glad this is a surviving episode. There's a LOT of detail and action to see and take in on this set.

Wow. That kidnapping plot was actually quite effective (not to mention *awesome*).

Apparently the fish people communicate in electronic warbling.

Ahhhhh, I see that suspension wire there...

Two appears to be wearing an earring. I'm going to assume that was part of his "sailor" disguise.

I'm not sure I buy Zaroff's "illness." After all, it's only the third episode and he hasn't said "NOTHING IN THE WORLD CAN STOP ME NOW" yet.

EXACTLY. SEE. NOW YOU'RE BEING STRANGLED.

POLLY, DON'T JUST STAND THERE WHILE HE HAS HIS BACK TO YOU. *DO* SOMETHING.

Well, close enouOH MY GOD DID ZAROFF JUST IMPALE THE PRIEST WITH A POLE I THINK HE DID HOLY SHIT

That image of the boys coming up with the fish masks seems to be One Of Those Images from this era that I see everywhere.

"Ben, you and I have other fish to fry. Come on!" ...Two...you did NOT just make that pun...

Oh wow. And Polly managed to escape completely on her own. Simple, but nice.

FIGHT SCENE! Oh wow, LOOK at Jamie dodge that sword! And suddenly he becomes the center of cling.

It's official: Zaroff is an Axe Crazy. You know how I know? Because he's bugfuck insane and he just shot the ruler of Atlantis.

"NOZING IN THE WORLD CAN STOP ME NOW!!!"

"The Underwater Menace, episode KILL THESE TWO MEN!!" #convenienttiming #what

Oh. So I guess Thous isn't dead after all. Good to know we still have someone sane to rule Atlantis.

Wow. Ben managed to get away with probably the least convincing guard-and-prisoner act ever.

"Do you know what you're doing?"
"Oh, what a question! Of COURSE I don't!"

Wait, WHAT was that about "closing night at Eddie Murphy's pub?"

Zaroff seems to be very unfortunately consistent in his counterattacks on Two's sabotage. Of course, he can't hold back the *ocean.*

AHA. NOW they've got him. And...Two wants to go BACK for him? Good ol' Doctor, I suppose.

Awwwww, and FYI Jaime, Polly will return the favor in the next story when you get a concussion on the moon.

So Two-and-Ben and Jamie-and-Polly have spent most of the episode separated and they both think that the others could be dead. Ouch.

"Any sign of the Doctor?"
"No. He must've died saving us."
"We'll raise a stone to him in the temple."
"No. No more temples. It was temples and priests and superstition that made us follow Zaroff in the first place. When the water finds its own level the temple will be buried forever. We shall never return to it, but we will have enough left to build a new Atlantis, without gods and without Fish People."
"Yes. That shall be his memorial."

Team Two is alive! Hug tiem nao.

Wow. Look at Jamie being all BAMF.

"You sound very happy, Jamie!"
"Oh aye, Doctor, I am now. You know, I never thought I'd say this but...well, it's great."
"What is?"
"Well, all this! Oh, I'll never know what makes it go, mind y', but... well at least I feel safe in here. It's only the wee things outside that're, well, alarming."

And with the TARDIS spinning wildly out of control, we return to the land of serial-to-serial cliffhangers!

I've heard that this serial gets a lot of flack for not being very good, but I actually enjoyed it. ESPECIALLY the surviving episode.

Originally Posted December 29th, 2010

THE MOONBASE

Written by Kit Pedler
Aired: February 11 – March 4, 1967

Apparently Troughton had Hartnell's title sequence for his first season. A much brighter version of it, too.

Hello, Ben and Polly! Wow, I never guessed Ben had such a heavy accent. Well, at least it'll be easy to tell all the men apart.

"That picture cannae be the moon! The moon's way up in the sky!" James. Robert. McCrimmon. I fucking love you.

I wouldn't be surprised if the sound effect for jumping on the moon turned out to be THE most insanely cartoony thing on this show.

And of course it wouldn't be a '60s science fiction show without a flying saucer or two!

Wait a sec..."let us collect our young friend"..."let me go see Jamie"... WHAT happened to him WHEN?

Or maybe he was that guy who was lying down with those markings that looked like Romana when she got bitten by the Alzarian spiders.

So according to 1966, we were just 100 years away from controlling the weather. From the moon.

Hey, that random guy sounds American!

Oh sure, kill off the black guy first.

Hey guys? Maybe you could...you know...TELL US what Jamie's doing instead of holding us in mostly silent suspense?

Or you could just let us stare at his partially exposed chest for a bit, I guess that works too.

"Where's Evans' body?"
"Over there."
So what's the betting that the cliffhanger is going to be "the body's missing"?

Called it. Okay, so it's not the cliffhanger, but the body IS missing.

"It's you...it's the Phantom Piper!" No Jamie, it's a Cyberman. You've got the coming-for-your-soul part about right, though.

OH WAIT A SEC THIS EPISODE IS AN ACTUAL EPISODE MADE OF FOOTAGE AND MOVING THINGS.

Wow. Jamie you are sweating like a madman.

Um, also you can stop yelling now. I think it's going to leave you alone.

Oh right, I'd COMPLETELY forgotten that Ben and Polly've not only seen the Cybermen before, but were there when they FIRST SHOWED UP.

"Stop this Cyberman nonsense! There were Cybermen, every child knows that, but they were all destroyed ages ago!"

"There are some corners of the universe which have bred the most terrible things, things which act against everything that we believe in. They must be fought!" Ah yes, that famous line. And I love how Two pronounces "evil" like "ee-ville."

So they have 24 hours to identify this mysterious virus aboard the base. Don't worry, there will be no Jack Bauer jokes forthcoming.

NOW he's claiming to be a doctor of medicine? Usually he denies that for some reason or another.

Between this and Seeds of Death, you'd think humanity would learn to NOT run the world by a single control center on the moon.

So I JUST realized that even though they have an international and interracial crew up there, there are no women. What is this bullshit.

Wow. I'm a little impressed with that French guy for taking so long to notice that Two was...what appeared to be trimming his pants.

AND HOW DID HE GET AWAY WITH TAKING THAT GUY'S SHOE OFF WITHOUT HIM NOTICING. Two, are you secretly a ninja?

Awww, Polly's taking such good care of Jamie OH MY GOD SHE JUST GOT ZAPPED IN THE HEAD BY A CYBERMAN.

It only just occurred to me how little sense it makes that Jamie should be this sick just from falling. Because, you know, IT'S THE MOON.

"Lister?"
"Well, you did say that you took your degree in Glasgow in 1888. Does seem an awful long time from now, 2070, or whatever it is."
"Polly, are you suggesting that I'm not confident to carry out these tests?"
"Oh no, no no no no! I was just wondering if there was anything that Joseph Lister didn't know in 1888 that might possibly help you now."

Approaching footsteps means... "It's Mr. Hobson! Out for blood! Ours! LOOK BUSY!"

omg moar cybermans

Nice spiderweb effect with the virus markings. I wonder if that was animated?

The virus is in the sugar? That would explain the really brief emphasis on it a couple minutes ago.

Back to reconstructions...and I couldn't even tell that there was a second Cyberman. Or who was trying to shoot it.

Wow. So apparently the Cybermen are leaving Jamie alone just because he has a head injury.

Well I have to admit, with the blurriness and the stark black-and-white contrast, the Cybermen actually look pretty scary here.

"Revenge...what is that?" So now I honestly have to ask, WHAT exactly is their motivation for killing everyone on Earth?

One of my Blog followers has that picture of Jamie with a headache as a *facepalm* icon. And now I know where it's from! #yayness

"They must have some weakness."
"They have, don't you remember? They can't stand radiation!"
So when did they introduce the gold allergy?

"Well in my day, we used to sprinkle witches with holy water." Jamie. C'mere. Is hug tiems nao.

I thought Ben was supposed to be a sailor, but he sure seems to know an awful lot about science.

Ben and Polly: Ready to fight Cybermen with nail varnish remover cocktails. Yes really.

Two seems to be talking to himself like he's 2 people. Probably why they keep switching back and forth between the same 2 shots of his face.

I'm AMAZED that the Cybermen haven't noticed yet that Two's tinkering with their control panels. Especially since he's talking to himself.

"Not you, Polly. This is men's work." Wut.

Attagirl Polly for not taking their crap!

Well, the Polly cocktail actually seems to be killing us some Cybermans.

"They must have failed."
"Yes."
"We must invade now."
Sorry, but I think The Invasion is another two seasons off.

So now that they've taken down the Cybermen in the base, why haven't they gotten back in touch with Earth?

checks the BBC photonovels I DID NOT REALIZE THAT CYBERMEN HAS CYBERSKELETONS THAT ACTUALLY LOOKED LIKE HUMAN BONES.

Huh. I would've liked to see this chase scene's real footage. I wonder how they imitated running in low gravity back then?

CYBERMANS ON THE MARCH.

"All resistance is useless." I see they went a step further. Not only is resistance useless, but ALL resistance is useless. *LE GASP*

Is it just me, or are parts of the Cybermen's outer joints made of wiffle balls?

And nobody's noticing Dr. Evans being all sketchy? Really? You're all too busy with your coffee?

I'm a little surprised that the pressure difference between the inside and outside of the base isn't tearing that hole bigger.

MAGICALLY FLYING CYBERMEN. Oh wait, sorry... SCIENTIFICALLY FLYING CYBERMEN.

And there was much rejoicing.

Off sneak the TARDIS crew...I have to admit, I like that they were still able to handle 3 companions, even if Jamie was sick half the time.

"Could that be them?"
"Possibly, and I hope it's the last we see of them."
Oh. Trust me. It isn't. It REALLY REALLY isn't.

"Doctor...LOOK!" THAT THERE BE A MACRA CLAW. Haven't seen those buggers since Gridlock.

Originally Posted July 10th, 2010

THE MACRA TERROR

Written by Ian Stuart Black
Aired: March 11 – April 1, 1967

FINALLY! TWO'S OPENING! Well, almost, we still have to get his theme variant in here.

Are we going to be hearing that pounding heartbeat/drumbeat throughout this whole episode? #herecomethedrums

Ah, looks like Jamie's finally been cleaned up and re-clothed.

What...if I didn't know better (which I probably don't), I'd say those were...elevator chorus girls?

"Well, this is gay. Why all the music?" Having a gay old time I suppose?

Suspicious Jamie is suspicious. Also clinging. (I might be restricting the Cling Counter to serials with more surviving episodes.)

Totally not Big Brother allegory right there. Nope. Totally not.

"Oh no, you're not gonnae do that to me! I'm no' a lassie!"
"Jamie, lasses've got ya!"

Aha, and now we have the origin of Polly's pixie cut.
AHAHAHAH, oh Ben, I've never seen you look so chill before. I mean...SUNGLASSES.

"Hey mister, would you call the ladies off? I'm frightened of what they might to do me." ....Jamie.

"But you look charming, sir!"
"That's what I'm frightened of!"
(There are no words for that last exchange. None.)

Okay, I'm pretty sure that's a telesnap of Salamander from The Enemy of the World they just used there.

NOBODY CLEANS DOCTOR TROUGHT. NOBODY.

Wow, Polly certainly seems to be fawning over Jamie. "Like a prince?" I sense impending jealous-Ben.

That was the most commanding "IT WILL BE FUN FOR ALL" I've ever heard in my life.

I don't think Ben and Polly are going to be very happy with Two for ruining their vacation.

Hang on, is it just me or is the Commander American? The accent doesn't sound completely British.

Is that a half-built rollercoaster off in the background? But I'll bet I know what those weird cries are...

Hello, Metal Gear Ray! I mean...Macra!

Ah yes, I think we know who the resident Law-Enforcing Douchebag of this serial is now.

What the controller just said was basically the non-Cybermen equivalent of "You shall be like us. You belong to us."

"THERE IS NO SUCH THING AS MACRA! MACRA DO NOT EXIST! THERE ARE NO MACRA!" #stop #hamtime

Oh. Brainwashed in your sleep. Lovely. Creepy.

Good ol' Jamie, he knows his evil voices when he hears them. On the other hand, WAKE UP, BEN!

I've seen the telesnaps of Ben and Polly sleeping in an icon before. I used to think it was adorable. Now I know better.

"The Doctor came into Polly's cubicle. She was fast asleep. The Doctor tried not to disturb her, but he had work to do." #notdodgyatall

To Jamie, everybody cling!

On a more serious note, s'ploding the wire doesn't seem to've snapped Ben out of his brainwashing.

Ahhhh yes, I recognize this picture.

"I take orders from no one but the Doctor!" #BAMFJamie

Ben Jackson: Now Grade-A Creeper.

OH HEY LOOK FOOTAGE! And that one telesnap of Ben and Polly looking terrified and clinging I've seen EVERYWHERE.

Well, good to know that even when he's brainwashed, Ben will still rush in and smash things trying to eat his girl.

Huh. I could've sworn that was an impending cliffhanger.

So that's what the controller really looks like. I recognize this shot, I know what's coming next.

"THEY'RE IN CONTROL! THEY'RE IN CONTROL!" ...Okay, I'll admit I wasn't quite expecting THAT.

"The strangers are being sent to you for pit labor! Put them in the Danger Gang!" That sounds like a group of punk comic book villains.

"Aye, well you don't send a lassie and an old man down to dig!"
"Old? What do you mean, old? I'm not old, Jamie!"

I think when one of your friends tells you "the voices tell me what to do," that's when you start worrying (if you aren't already.) They established a while ago that putting their masks and things on was pretty important so...why haven't they done it yet?

"No one must assume that the relative connection is constant." Then maybe you shouldn't be saying it out loud.

Good ol' Doctor, solving problems by doing science to them. Or, in this case, math.

Woah. When did the music turn 8-bit?

"Hey wait! Don't leave me down here!" You know, Polly, you could just...I dunno...follow him instead of just standing there.

Wait. Jamie. What are you wearing. Where did those silver overalls come from. (Unless that's the mining uniform...)

Awww, poor Ben doesn't know whether to listen to his own instincts or the creepy voices in his head.

"But the voices are here to help us! They are our friends!" #creepy

Jamie finds a Macra and thinks he knows a solution: bung a rock at it.

Hang on, if they're not going to pour the gas in to try and kill Jamie, then what's this "other reason" that Two speaks of?

"Because there's something trapped down there they wish to keep alive!" Ah. That's why.

Oh neat, they even got a bit of a gas effect in there!

Trapped on both sides by giant monsters? Believe it or not, I know what that feels like.

So apparently my "I made you a TARDIS, but I breakeded it" macro wasn't a picture of the TARDIS after all.

And Jamie is saved, thanks to the power of FRESH AIR!

Yikes. Hello, Unexpected Pep Rally.
HOW MUCH STEROIDS IS THEIR COACH ON.

Unexpected Jamie...WAIT. IS THIS THE SCENE WHERE HE
TEACHES THE HIGHLAND FLING.

It is. Oh god yes. (but seriously, what has the coach been smoking)

Oh. Well that didn't last very long.

Oh wow. The telesnap where Ben turns Jamie over makes it look like
he's about to cry.

"Jamie, I'm..." Looks like I wasn't that far off.

"This stranger would still be a danger to all of us!" STRANGER
DANGER.

Want to bring down a tyrant? Just yell at his giant face on a screen.

"Stop! You're breaking the law!"
"Bad laws were made to be broken!"

The Macra seem to be in full-on "PAY NO ATTENTION TO THE
MAN BEHIND THE CURTAIN" mode now.

Four minutes? What a coincidence, that's about how much time they
have left in the episode.

"Ben, we've got very little time! It's all up to you!" REDEMPTION
TIME!

And then there was a negative s'plosion!

Aaaaaand there's that annoying marching music from the beginning
of the serial...

Aww, and just when Two gets another cool hat he has to make an
escape plan to keep from becoming the next leader of the Colony.

Stealth through dance. Team Two thinks of everything.

Originally Posted January 7th, 2011

THE FACELESS ONES

Written by David Ellis and Malcolm Hulke
Aired: April 8 – May 13, 1967

Huh. They still haven't started the Troughton variation of the theme tune yet.

Malcolm Hulke! Nice to see his name in the writer's credits again.

"IT'S A FLYING BEASTIE!" Now all we have to do is hope that this will be better airport/airplane-oriented story than Time-Flight.

Ah yes, and of course everyone's natural instinct is to run very fast from a plane that's already airborne and isn't going to land on them.

"SCATTER!" *lose Ben* ...there are times on this show when fail is a beautiful thing.

"Jamie, come over here with me!" Aww, poor little confused!Jamie. WAIT WHAT HAPPENED TO THE MUSIC.

Jumping right into mysterious deaths and secret passageways. Making haste on the plot, then, are we?

Guys, I'm highly doubting that Polly would've heard your whispered shouting in such a noisy area. Really.

"Doctor! I've just seen a man killed!"

"By one of the beasties?"
That was funny until I realized why it really really wasn't.

Jamie, I see your hand there. You're just a natural comforter, aren't you? (or creeper, or clinger, take your pick) Awwwww...

So THAT'S where the Manly Side-By-Side thing of Two and Jamie came from. Like the sleeping thing from The Macra Terror, it's creepy now.

Over on Tumblr, we call this Jamie being AMAZED AND PERPLEXED (yes, the all-caps are intentional).

Cling cling cling, and I'm VERY convinced that the attendant here is in league with the creepers from earlier.

NO BEN, DON'T GO IN THAT DOOR.

"Yes! She saw the man killed!"
"He was electrocuted with a ray gun!"
How many times has Two had to give Jamie a hush-you jab so far?

Regardless of the actual emergency, I'm finding that the TARDIS crews' struggles with modern-day authorities are always the most relatable.

Now there's a mysterious scaly arm sticking out of a cabinet. That can't be good.

I'm sorry to say it, but if I was in that guy's position right now, I wouldn't believe Two and Jamie either.

Ah, hello Unexpected!Polly. Don't tell me you've been brainwashed again...

Aaaaaaaand you have. Great.

Having never been there, I can't tell exactly which parts of this serial were filmed at Gatwick and which parts were done in the studio.

Although I can certainly hazard a few guesses.

I'm not sure your story's going to hold much water if it's your "first visit to England" despite having an excellent English accent.

And thankfully, Two calls her on it. Complete with a snippet of surviving footage.

"Jamie, I don't think we're very welcome here. When I say 'run,' we run."

("Jamie's is a foreign newspaper, and also upside down.") Two and Jamie: Masters of Disguise.

I think Two just demonstrated why shady groups in fiction need to stop giving themselves cover names that hint at their true intentions.

Huh. Looks like Ben's ploy from earlier with pretending to be a new member of the airport staff got him out of trouble after all.

How is this show so damn good at making things so consistently creepy?

Ah yes, the old trip-them-up-by-making-them-reveal-the-detail-you-didn't-mention maneuver.

It looks like the boys are all climbing into a photo booth...OH WAIT THEY ACTUALLY ARE. #goddamnburninators #iwantedtoseethis

"What is this place?"
"It's a machine that takes your photograph."
"Photograph?"
"Well y'see, you've got your..."
"Not now."

Poor Jamie. Lost, confused, but still oh-so-adorable. #AMAZEDANDPERPLEXED

Hello Samantha Briggs! Might I say it's a pleasure to finally meet you but what do you even have on your head.

So THAT'S what a Liverpool accent sounds like.

"ONE STEP CLOSER AND I'LL BLOW YOU ALL TO SMITHEREENS!" Not sure I even want to think what would happen if you did that in an airport today.

OH GOD POLLY I'M GOING TO BE SEEING THAT FACE IN MY NIGHTMARES TONIGHT HOLY SHIT

So Jamie only gets to introduce Samantha as "this young lady" whom he wants him to meet. I wonder how Two will interpret that...

Aww, Jamie is a good obedient little puppy, always does what Two tells him.

TROUGHTSICLE!

Ah, THERE'S Pat's theme tune!

And so Two's hankie must be sacrificed for the greater good (but considering how much he keeps in his pocket, he probably has a ton more).

Yup, see? OH NOT THE COAT.

Oh god. Pat freezing on the floor. I don't care that he was faking it. My heart was break.

And now what is his hair. That frost must've melted fast, because it looks like he just got out of the shower.

Creeper!Two be creepin'.

Also, I just had another one of my Awkward Fanartist Moments when I realized how much I've been drawing Jamie's face wrong.

Did Two just call it "Comedian Tours"?

"I believe Chameleon Tours to be merely a front! A cover!"
"For what?"
DRAMATIC CLOSE-UP "For the mass kidnapping of young people!"

Still sounds like he's saying "Comedian Tours."

"I think we're dealing with people who are not from this planet."
"Oh that hardly answers my queWHAT DID YOU SAY."

Two just turned a teacup to ice with a space pen to prove a point. This show.

The Cling: No One is Immune. (But seriously, every time Jamie puts his arm around someone, I need a multiverse for my d'awwwws.)

I think the Commandant and the inspector have the exact same glasses. No wonder I keep getting them mixed up.

Also, I understand completely why they wanted Samantha Briggs to come on as the next companion. She's got spunk and she knows how to use it.

...and yet when Jamie gets arms put around him (that aren't the Doctor's, apparently), he puts on a pouty-face.

The quick turn-arounds for the planes made no sense to me until I remembered that they're in England. #americafail

More Unexpected!cling, except this one was actually done with malicious intent. Dun dun DUN.

Must not make "problem, officer?" joke...

I just realized that I might've had Jamie's shoes, or something like them. *looks at the box of mis-ordered shoes I haven't sent back yet*

What. That flight attendant is existing in my mind as an amalgamation of several companions: Tegan, Dodo, Susan, and a little of Vicki.

Also, that airplane looks a lot more roomy and comfortable than the one I was on earlier today. #the60s

People in airplane cockpits with guns pointed at them. As a New Yorker, this situation is becoming more and more unsettling.

So of COURSE it's the second-to-last canister that Two tries to rip off the shelf that turns out to open the secret passageway.

NO SERIOUSLY, HOW IS THIS SERIAL DOING SUCH A
GOOD JOB AT CREEPING ME OUT.

"Doctor!"

"He's dead. You're coming with me."

"I'll not leave him."

"You have five seconds to change your mind."

Don't bother. He won't.

Sadly, the combined might of Scot and Sam is not enough to conquer
the Creeper.

...who now appears to be thinking "why should I kill them one at a
time with a little gun, when I can kill them all WITH A BIGGER
GUN? :D"

Oh. No. No he's not. He's actually not doing the moving-the-laser-
beam-slowly-towards-his-captives thing. That's only for Bond villains.

And of COURSE he just leaves them alone without seeing if they
actually die. #somanytropesicanteven

From the way this scene is going, I'm going to bet that they get saved
by a pocket hand mirror.

WHY HELLO HOT AND SWEATY JAMIE.

Yup, I was right: saved by a pocket hand mirror. SCIENCE. I mean...
COSMETICS.

I just realized that the nurse kinda looks like Barbara a little bit. What.

Jamie: Human Clingwrap. Two: Gallifreyan Crutch.

Apparently, side-effects of your Gallifreyan Crutch include fictional
rare tropical diseases.

"My two friends became involved with Chameleon Tours and they've
both disappeared!" And it's their last story, too!

He just...kissed her...to steal her ticket...JAMIE MCCRIMMON I would've thought better of you than to take advantage of a lady like that!

Jeez, is that your response to everything? Point a gun at it?

"How high can fighters go these day, commandant?"
"Oh, ten miles plus."
"How futile."
I think I know where this thread is going.

Oh god. That flight attendant has quite an *epic* creeperface.

Poor Jamie, nobody warned him about the side-effects of air travel on one's health.

Uh oh, looks like somebody's airsick (presumably they explained before take-off that the restrooms were at the back of the cabin).

These back-and-forth communications with the fighter jet are starting to give me flashbacks to Dr. Strangelove for some reason.

Wow. I thought the airplane would be docking with a spaceship, but apparently it IS the spaceship.

Also, it looks like being in the restroom saved Jamie from being whatever-happened-to-the-other-passengers'd.

Ah, so it's docking with a spaceship anyway. I figured.

"The intelligence of Earth people is comparable only to that of animals on our planet." Oh boy, I love being looked down upon by aliens.

Jamie McCrimmon, a-creepin' he will go...

Oh. Um, hello Close-Up of Jamie's Eyes.

Miniature people "like dolls" in cabinets? Huh. Looks like these guys got a jump on the Master's TCE technology.

I find it interesting that it's Two doing all the social investigative work at Gatwick while Jamie is trying to get things done UP IN SPACE.

Ah. FINALLY we get our explanation for what the everloving crap has actually been going on.

Eww. Blobby puddle of blob.

So now Two finally learns where Jamie went, and it's OFF TO THE RESCUE!

"Sure the Doctor will think 'o some way of rescuing us?"
"Not this time, Jamie."
Oh, you just wait.

"I am the director." ...uh oh.

Two, I know you want to get on that last plane, but I don't think you really count as a "young person."

I'm not gonna lie, I won't be remotely surprised if Captain Blade is still suspicious of chameleon!Two.

Ohhhhhhhhh crap they've got Jamie. AND THEY TOOK AWAY HIS SCOTTISH ACCENT. WHAT IS THIS.

BEN. POLLY. THIS IS YOUR LAST EPISODE. NOW MIGHT BE A GOOD TIME TO SHOW UP AGAIN.

"I checked with the medical center. You're both human." But didn't you just confer with the director and Jamie about who the Doctor was?

People of the airport, RALLY 'ROUND! We're going hunting for survivors.

"Well I don't think you've done a good job on him... You've lost his Scots accent in the process! I much preferred the original."

Hmm, Two seems to be going for a divide-and-conquer tactic here. Pretty handy, since it would involve the destruction of a bunch of people.

Uh oh, they're contacting the airport for proof when they haven't found the originals yet. Somehow I don't see this ending well.

Looks like the Doctor was already a good hand at screwdrivers before he decided it could be a bit more sonic.

"You haven't averted your fate, only postponed it." But yes he has.

So the originals were hidden inside cars the whole time? That doesn't sound like a place where they'd "never be found."

FINALLY Blade sort of stops being a dick and turns his gun on his boss.

Ahhhhh, so THAT'S where that "in the closet" icon came from.

("He's off, leaving Jamie and Samantha feeling awkward.") Oh, I know where this is going.

"I must go. The Doctor'll be...well, your brother'll be here any moment!"
"Yah. Well, ta-ta, then." *smooch*
Awwwww...

I wonder if this is the last, or one of the last, group shots we'll ever get of the first Team Two.

"It's as if we've never been away!"
"...You really want to go, don't you?"
"Well, we won't leave, Doctor, if you really need us."
D':

"Alright then, off you go. Now go on, Ben can catch his ship and become an Admiral and...you, Polly, you can look after Ben."

I look at this prolonged image of the telesnap of Polly and Jamie's last hug and...I almost feel like I'm *in* it.
#multiverseformydaaaawwws

("And so with a final backward glance, Ben and Polly walk out of the hanger and out of the Doctor's life.") Tearing up a little here, guys.

"Well, I didn't tell the others but, we've lost the TARDIS." Wait WHAT.

"You mean somebody's stolen it?!"
"I don't know, but that's what we're going to find out! Come on..."
manly stride

Ben, Polly, just a month ago I barely knew you, but now I've
completed your run. It was short, but it was a good one. Take care,
you two...

(...and next we'll get to join our lovely Space Husbands on the hunt
for their former bachelor pad.)

Originally Posted January 20th, 2011

CHARACTER RETROSPECTIVE: BEN AND POLLY

One of the unfortunate side-effects of The Lost Episodes is that you get a few companions who are grossly underrated because of limited availability. In other words, we need to complete more of Two's earliest stories so that more fans can fall in love with the excellence that is Ben and Polly. I can tell you it was a delightfully surreal experience to come back to my Lancaster dorm after a day in Newcastle to learn that another episode of The Underwater Menace had been recovered (as of this writing, I still haven't seen it). On the other hand, it's nice that their one complete surviving serial is their introductory story, so it's still possible to "meet them" properly. But enough about technicalities: I love Ben and Polly.

Like Barbara before her, I wrote about Polly in a paper for school, and upon reflection I think I gave her a bad rap. I was describing the female companions in broad strokes and I put Polly in the "Screamer" category because I didn't think she fit in any of the others. But in retrospect, I put Donna in the "Intellectuals" category because she was her own unique breed of smart, and so was Polly. Polly is incredibly adaptable, and her main strength comes from her fantastic social and problem-solving skills. She's the first to believe the effects of the Doctor's very first regeneration, she talks easily with just about anyone, and she always has her heart in the right place. Polly never accepts Being A Woman as a weakness, especially when she's told that something is "man's work." I once read an article about how the Magical Girl genre of Japanese manga and anime was built around "weaponized femininity," and sometimes I think Polly might be right at home in such a series. After all, this is the girl who once helped defeat the Cybermen with a nail-polish-remover cocktail. On the moon. I could easily see her shooting energy beams forged from the Power of Love and Friendship and look really awesome while doing it. And speaking of friendship...

Considering Ben and Jamie are the only two male companions to travel with the Doctor at the same time, I'm a little surprised the show didn't do more with them being bros. Then again, Ben's main focus always seemed to be keeping Polly safe. Somehow I think he and Harry Sullivan might've gotten along pretty well, given their shared navy background and the fact that they were both more "heart" than "head," unlike Steven Taylor. Ben is kind of a man's-man-to-be: an action guy who always has to save the girl, but had assorted moments of failing adorably. Come to think of it, Ben being manly in general is pretty adorable. I find it fascinating that, even though he and Polly don't really know each other before they join up with the Doctor, they still come across almost as couple-like as Ian and Barbara before them. Like with the Coal Hill School teachers, most post-departure spin-off material of them I've read, and listened to, comes to the same conclusion: that they do wind up together. Although even *The Sarah Jane Adventures* never explicitly stated that they got married, they definitely wound up as partners in some form. There's even a moment in the Big Finish audio "The Five Companions" where Polly is asked if she "sees any of Ben these days," to which she replies that she sees "all of him, every day."

Speaking of which, earlier in that same scene Polly is bemoaning that she didn't contribute much to the team besides making tea and coffee, to which the Fifth Doctor reassures her that she was an active and invaluable member of the crew. And that brings me to her actress, Anneke Wills. At my very first Doctor Who convention (Regenerations 2011 in Wales), Anneke was on the first panel after the opening ceremonies. The first five minutes of the panel involved Anneke clearing the air of some negative rumors and then standing up and proclaiming "you know what? Enough is enough, I'm taking the power back!" My jaw dropped, the room burst into cheers and applause, and within a minute the panel was chugging along on its merry way. All I could think was, "oh my god, with an opening like that, this weekend is going to be *awesome*." Sometime the next day, as I was standing on line for an autograph panel, she passed by a few feet from me and I caught her attention. I had to thank her for her awesome speech the day before.

"Hi, can I just say…this is my very first Doctor Who convention and I could not possibly have asked for a more awesome opening than what you gave us yesterday."

She took my hands in hers and gazed lovingly at me as I said this, and then thanked me in return. Then she asked me if I was having a good time.

Absolutely.

THE EVIL OF THE DALEKS

Written by David Whitaker
Aired: May 20 – July 1, 1967

So we open with our two wonderful gents chasing desperately after the truck that's pinched their ride. Needless to say, this fails.

"Oh, foreign, is he?"
"ME foreign? YOU'RE the one that's foreign, I'm Scottish!"

Huh. Someone appears to be listening in.

The note's signed "J. Smith"? Hmmmmm, I wonder...

Wait Two just pushed Jamie back into the cabinets from the last story and then they vanished what

And now we switch to...two random guys doing science to it, apparently.

So I definitely heard the name "Waterfield" mentioned, but I can't place exactly where or when these guys are.

This explanation of "what are trains" has been interrupted by Escaping Bad Guy.

Ahhh, the bar. I remember the bar.

"Now, don't give up, Doctor. Remember Bruce."
"Bruce?"
"Robert Bruce!"
...who?

Now THIS is interesting: apparently the matches that Two's using as a clue was planted there by the Creepers of the Week. #twosclues

Woah. Hello, Mysterious Science Room.

So I wonder what's so significant about that little statue...

"This is his assistant and secretary, Mr. James McCrimmon."
I feel less concerned with how he knows this and more with secretary!Jamie.

To reiterate: SECRETARY!JAMIE. #weirdimages

Ah, so the dude with the epic sideburns (or are those mutton chops?) IS Mr. Waterfield.

"Nobody knows the trouble I've seen, nobody knows my sorrow..." plays the radio as Jamie sits drowning his woes in drink.

Not gonna lie, I fansqueed when I first saw this telesnap.

"I've done everything that you've asked of me. Isn't that enough?"
Oh. I bet I know where this is going.

GEE, HE WOULDN'T'VE HAPPENED TO'VE BEEN TALKING TO...*GASP* A DALEK, WOULD HE?

WAIT. MORE IMPORTANTLY. IS THAT JAMIE JAMMING OUT WITH GIRLS IN MINI-SKIRTS TO "PAPERBACK WRITER."

Even better, it comes in right before the line "and his clinging wife doesn't understand." UTTER. GLORIOUS. PERFECTION.

ogling "Oh, if only the laird could see that..."

"Jamie, I'm being stared at. Is there something wrong with me?" I. This. I can't even.

"Is my hair in disarray?"

"What? No more than usual."

"Do I look, erm, strange and bizarre?"

"Eh, well maybe I'm used to you."

#somarried

I wouldn't advise doing science to it if you don't know what any of the buttons do.

DALEK. UP IN THIS.

...is it just me, or do the Daleks have slight accents this time?

"It's half-past the nine 'o clock!" THE nine 'o clock, Jamie?

I kinda love how Troughton's voice is so well-suited to talking low but still sounding awesome.

The good news: Mr. Waterfield is BAMF enough to talk down to a Dalek. The bad news: he clearly has NO IDEA what's he's getting himself into.

Um, okay, Jamie, why are you clinging to the random stranger you just met?

So I wonder what the significance of ripping Two's photo and putting it in the box was...

...ah. Wow, this story really has no shortage of unusually intricate plots, doesn't it?

Knocked out, teleported, and...wake up on a sunny day with birds chirping outside. Huh. I can think of worse fates.

Oh wow. Maxtible's beard grows into his hair. It's a mane. HE'S A LION.

VICTORIA! This is the first time I've seen you outside of Tomb of the Cybermen!

"YOU. HAVE. NOT. EA-TEN. YOU. WILL. EAT. THAT. IS AN. OR-DER." DALEK SAYS THERE ARE STARVING CHILDREN IN AFRICA WHO WOULD LOVE THIS FOOD.

Huh. Since when do Daleks care so much about human weight?

Slightly amused that it was the mention of static electricity that caught Two's attention. So, when DON'T the Daleks run on static?

Okay, there were the ones with the panels in Dalek Invasion of Earth, but OTHER than that.

Waaaaaaait a sec...since *when* have the Daleks known about Jamie?

Guys. Pat's face. It is seriously the most amazing thing. His expression when the Dalek came in was just...I can't even...

Ohhhhh crap. Rassilon himself be damned if Two's going to let the Daleks do anything to Jamie.

Uh, Jamie, while you're busy getting yourself up to speed, you might want to pay attention to the man behind the curtain. #worldofcreep

Okay. Seriously. WHAT was up with that random guy sneaking in and abducting Jamie?

Ack. Cliffhanger with a close-up on a Dalek sucker. ...Ack.

Well now, let's see if we can't learn the identity of this week's Mr. Creeper who's kidnapped Jamie.

Wait, his boss said he didn't send him then wibbly-wobbly things and now he doesn't remember and he's looking for Victoria what?

And now Two's shown up so...I guess that whole subplot was completely unnecessary?

Jamie seems just as confused as I am, though.

"DO. NOT. BE. A-FRAID. YOU. ARE. NOT. TO BE. EX-TER-MIN-A-TED." Aww, that's actually nice reassurance from a Dalek.

I'd just like to say how adorably cliche it is that Victoria is shown as the captive girl sitting in her cell feeding birds through the bars.

Maybe Two is just sucking up to Mr. Waterfield for facade's sake, but it almost sounds like he's selling Jamie out.

Jamie is not dumb, you bearded twat.

Oh wait...he wasn't talking about Jamie at all. So, who's this Random Ethnic Dude?

Ah, yes. They did mention something about another serial than Tomb of the Cybermen having one of these ethnic-strongman-servant types.

Ohhhh, I see. That guy's going to be the guard Jamie has to fight to get to Victoria.

For some reason, I'm really loving this dramatic piano music.

"YOU. HAVE. TRA-VELED. TOO. MUCH. THROUGH. TIME. YOU. ARE. MORE. THAN. HU-MAN." ...it's taken you THIS long to notice that?

I think this is the first time I've ever heard Patrick Troughton say "Skaro." And I just realized why.

Huh, there's that random guy who had his memories scrambled earlier. I wonder what he wants now.

Aww, Jamie's such a little gentleman with the housemaid. Even insists she call him by his real name and not "sir."

But he's not interested in history lessons from Two, no matter how many light brigades he's seen charge.

I would call this a little spat, but it actually sounds like Serious Business now.

Wow. Jamie's so worked up that he needs some alone time. This is going to sound strange but, I never really pictured him as the type.

"I won't have you ruining everything trying to rescue Victoria Waterfield!" Okay now I wonder if Two's just using reverse psychology on him.

In all seriousness, this is shaping up to look almost like one of Seven's plots, not Two's. Unless I'm really missing something.

Apparently I'm not. Two was in fact using reverse psychology to get Jamie to cooperate. Two, I'm ashamed. This is too underhanded for you.

Also, I still don't understand the point of that random ruffian who keeps showing up.

"IT. IS. FOR. YOU. DOC-TOR. TO. SELECT. THE. MA-JOR. FEEL-INGS. TO. MAKE. UP. THIS. HU-MAN. FAC-TOR." I bet I know what he'll pick.

(since this is the Doctor we're talking about, he's bound to pick the ones based on love and kindness and so on :3)

And so begins Jamie's test...

Ah, and there's the creeper guy from earlier come to loot the house, but then DALEK.

Footage! Although I wonder if that was made specially for the recon.

Wait...that's the door with the spikes falling out of the ceiling, isn't it.

It is! But naturally Jamie survives. Because JAMIE.

A CHALLENGER APPEARS. As does the cliffhanger.

FAHDFHALSFHKLSDAHFL GUYS. I KNOW TEST PATTERNS LOOK RETRO. BUT CONSIDER THE PEOPLE WHO ARE WATCHING THIS WITH HEADPHONES. HIGH. PITCH. FUCK.

And now we return to Jamie McCrimmon vs. the Unfortunate Ethnic Stereotype. Complete with Snippets of Surviving Footage!

And the winner is...JAMIE MCCRIMMON! #surprisesurprise

With those shadows, it REALLY looks like Jamie suddenly has a beard.

Awww, and Jamie's going to be a good wee laddie and rescue the bad man from falling to his death.

Wait...is it just me, or do I open a lot of my Jamie-related Tweets with "awwww"? (it would make sense, though)

I'm...not sure what just happened. He shoved Jamie onto the bed, threatened him, then helped him up and lead him away...what?

"If you want the Human Factor, a part of it must include mercy." Good ol' Doctor...

Ohhhhh, I get it. The guy didn't shove Jamie before, he was pushing him out of the way of that giant axe.

"Hey hey, now come on, we'll have none of that! We have to be friends, d'y'hear? Frrrriends."
"...:)"
"Aye."

"We'll go together. There's NO ONE I'd rather have with me." Wow. Jamie's still REALLY mad at Two to say something like that, isn't he?

Mr. Waterfield's really turning out to be a major coward. On the other hand, I think he's hearing voices now.

"Near the end now, you've done enough..." PUT THAT GUN DOWN.

NO. SERIOUSLY. WHO IS THAT OTHER GUY.

"She's very beautiful, Kemel." Aww, and Jamie's already in love (see what I mean about the "awwww"s?)

I think this is the first time I've ever heard Jamie whisper.

Yikes. Maybe it's just the brainwashing or whatever it is, but this guy is being a MASSIVE asshole to that maid.

Actually Maxtible, you were onto something with the whole "being afraid of the Daleks" thing.

"For centuries now, men have searched for the greatest secret of all." You mean the Answer to Life, the Universe, and Everything? It's 42.

Oh wait, he just wants to learn the secret of alchemy and turn metals into gold. Fair enough.

New way to defeat a Dalek: grab some rope, throw it around the front, and pull it into a fireplace. Explosions and gurgling may ensue.

"Miss Waterfield, can y' open the door? We've come to get you!" But then DALEK.

They're really having fun with this defeating-Daleks-with-rope thing, aren't they?

Security before introductions. Jamie, I'm not sure if you're being gentlemanly or just cool.

"Oh, uh, Jamie McCrimmon. I came to give you this." I was half expecting him to say "I'm Jamie McCrimmon, I'm here to rescue you." #starwars

So it looks like this mysterious creeper guy might be a robot or android after all.

"I am not a student of human nature. I am a professor of a much wider academy of which human nature is merely a part." The Doctor > you.

Oh goody, more jewel-based hypnotism.

On an unrelated note, is it just me or are Maxtible's glasses always horribly askew?

Oh. Oh. PLEASE TELL ME THE TAME!DALEKS ARE COMING UP SOON. THEY SOUND SO ADORABLE.

"DOC-TOR. BE. CARE-FUL." Aww, the Dalek's worried about him (for some odd reason).

I have to admit, Two's taking a pretty big gamble here. Of course, that could just prove how much faith he has in human nature.

Jamie is being so consistently awesome in this story and I love it.

For instance, it appears that he could kick your ass with a chair.

AND NOW HE APPEARS TO BE SWORDFIGHTING. *remembers that one Short Trip where he fights zombies with a claymore* #noreally #hedoes

Oh wait, that guy wasn't a robot, he just had a Dalek control device on him.

Jamie won't even let Two touch him. Again, Serious Business.

"NO, Doctor! Look, I'm telling you this: you and me, we're...we're finished! You're just too callous for me." ...D':

Theeeeeeere we go. Already the Cling has returned.

"Jamie...they're taking me for a ride! Jamie, they're playing a game! It's a game!" Awwwww, tame!Daleks want to play!

"Oh, I'm dizzy...oh, I'm dizzy..."
"DIZZ-Y? DIZZ-Y? DIZZ-Y DOC-TOR!"
scratches the Daleks behind their non-existent ears

Pat actually sounded a little like Hartnell just there. Also, PLAYING PARENT TO LITTLE-CHILDREN!DALEKS. I CAN'T EVEN. #AWWWWWW

"WHO. IS. THIS?"
"Oh this is Jamie, he's a friend!"
"FRIEEEEND. HE-LLO, FRIEEEEEND!"
aksljfklsajfkldsfkldasfhkls

Guys. The Daleks have legit vocal inflections now. It...this...I love this. So much.

HE IS BEING THEIR PRESCHOOL TEACHER YOU GUYS
AND HE'S NAMING THEM AND TEACHING THEM ABOUT
FRIENDSHIP AND YES

Awwww, funtime's over now. :(
Wait...HOW did you just "forget" Victoria in the secret passage?

Increasingly suspicious Mr. Waterfield is increasingly suspicious.
And then there was a s'plosion!

"Don't worry, Kemel, I shall protect you." Awww...

"You mean just walk into the city?" One does not simply walk into
Skaro.

Yes Dalek, I think you've made it quite clear that there is an
emergency and that there are humans in the city.

PAT WHERE DID YOUR EYES GO

Oh wow. The tame!Daleks talking about the Doctor being his friend
doesn't sound adorable anymore. Now it's creepy.

Wait...what...did Maxtible just have a seizure or something?

"What is your name?"
"O-ME-GA."
Several seasons from now, that won't sound so welcoming.

"You don't think I know my own mark? That wasn't Omega at all!"
Ah. I was wondering why he'd started speaking without inflections.

"Look at the size 'o THAT thing!" #yesjamieitISabigone

They seem to be title-dropping several other Dalek serials (made and
unmade) but not the one they're actually in.

Two, you might want to turn your overconfidence down a notch or
so. Also, you look like you have streaks of blood running down your
face.

I still don't understand how discovering the Human Factor helped to identify the Dalek Factor, especially since it seems so very obvious.

Also, it's interesting seeing the Dalek Emperor all the way back here, considering I first saw him over a year ago in New Who.

(Back then I thought the name was just a gimmick to make them sound more powerful or cool, but now I know it was actual continuity. Sorta.)

FINALLY THE LAST EPISODE.

I think it shows how much Jamie's growing that he considers alchemy "an old wives' tale."

AWWWW THERE'S HIS POUTY-FACE.

Hellooooo, what's this about Two considering taking everyone back to Gallifrey?

"Human beings...into Daleks." So it's like Jubilee, but more literal.

So I wonder if Maxtible's being truthful or just faking it. At this point I think either choice is fair game.

Oh. I see what you did there. JAMIE-BOY. YOUR MASTER NEEDS YOUR HELP. FETCH.

Incidentally, Maxtible what is your face.

Now I can only assume that Two is faking this.

Ah yes, the ol' switcheroo.

"DIZZ-Y. DIZZ-Y. DIZZ-Y DA-LEKS. DIZZ-Y. DIZZ-Y. DIZZ-Y DA-LEKS." OH MY GOD I THINK THEY'RE SINGING YOU GUYS

omg. The way they're all babbling "whyyy?" kinda reminds me of Elmira in those old Tiny Toon segments. #mychildhood

Apparently that was Alpha who just unleashed a small can 'o whoop-ass on one of the Dalek controllers.

Uh oh, I think Mr. Waterfield just got exterminated.

STOP CHANTING "KILL" REPEATEDLY LIKE THAT IT'S CREEPY AS BALLS OH GOD

Maxtible, I think you can just die now. You've more than served your purpose to this story.

Wow. Daleks be s'plodin' all over the place.

"Where is my father? Is he dead?"
"Yes. Yes, I'm afraid he is, but he didn't die in vain. I think we've seen the end of the Daleks forever."

NO

YOU

HAVEN'T.

"The end. The final end." #lies

Originally Posted January 30th, 2011

THE TOMB OF THE CYBERMEN

Written by Kit Pedler and Gerry Davis
Aired: September 2-23, 1967

Oh, Pat's titles. How long has it been? Not since...the last time I watched an Every Doctor Who Opening video.

"Well, what do you think?"
"I don't know! I can't believe it! It's so big!"
VICTORIA! I haven't seen you since...the last time I saw this!

Also, the less said about how *massive* a double-entendre that last tweet was, the better.

"Try to give us a smooth take-off, Doctor." JAMIE. Cling-counter: 1

Yeah, thanks the influence of my Tumblr friends, I'm compelled to count the number of Two/Jamie clingings in this story :3

Huh. The music turned off when they turned the detonation knob down. And then there was a quarry-s'plosion!

Just like The Moonbase, this has a remarkably diverse crew for the time, including nationality, race, and...FINALLY A WOMAN!

"Look at him. 'Archeologist' written all over him." Actually, he points and laughs at archeologists. Wait...archeologist? Two? Seriously?

Jamie, I fail to understand how you could've "not had much exercise lately" while traveling with the Doctor.

Is anyone else less-than-okay with the fact that the one person labeled a "servant" here is a black guy? Racefail much?

Hand-holding! Cling-counter: 2.

"You look very nice in that dress, Victoria."
"Thank you. Don't you think it's a bit..."
"A bit short? Oh I shouldn't worry about that, look at Jamie's."
"Hey, I'll have you know that...oh, aye!"

The woman with the giant hair and the accent practically SCREAMS "secretly a bad guy." It's been a while, so I honestly don't remember.

Wobbly sets are wobbly. #pointlessobservationispointless

"We do not need any other protection now that you are with us." Or she could just be hitting on that other guy.

"I wonder what this is." That, my dear Victoria, appears to be a BFG: a Big Fucking Gun.

"Revitalizing is just what I need." WAIT. NO. VICTORIA. DON'T GET IN THAT THING.

Whew. Okay. Good. That was close.

Raising caterpillars? Oh hello cybermat!

That giant glowing wheel with the dial in the front control room kinda looks like something from a game show...

AGH VICTORIA WHY DID YOU GET BACK IN THAT THING NOW YOU'RE TRAPPED.

And apparently I was right about that woman being a villain.

Uh oh, and now Jamie's falling victim to the giant hypno-wall.

AND THEN THERE WAS A CYBERMAN.

So that Cyberman was just a mock-up after all. I thought it coming out on a track like that was just a little odd.

"It's certainly inactive, but it's not a fossil." And out comes the 500 Year Diary!

Putting the cybermat in your bag. Umm...yeah, smart move, Victoria.

I'm a bit surprised Jamie and Victoria aren't taking up the offer to spend the night in the TARDIS, considering all the crazy. Then again...

"Hey, let the Doctor pass or I'll..."
Toberman grabs the Doctor's shirt
"...yes, well, let the Doctor pass."

The hatch is open! Time to traverse into the titular tomb...

Ah yes, welcome to Meals of the Future, Victoria.

I wonder if we'll ever find out what the coffee was drugged with, but I'll bet it's the cybermat making Victoria drowsy right now.

On the other hand, Weird Accent Lady did say "you've *barely* touched your coffee,'" so maybe Victoria did get drugged.

Is Cyberman melting tiems nao?

Cling-count: 3 (although that was completely expected and justified, so maybe it doesn't count)

Awww, wook at da widdle cyburmat. Scoot scoot scoot...

And the Cybermen emerge from their entombment, in that sequence that even scared the crap out of Peter Davison as a child. I can see why...

Victoria Waterfield: Shooter of Cybermats. Oh hells yeah.

"You belong to uzzz. You shall be like uzzz."

"Then why close the hatch on them? It doesn't make sense, Vic."
"I didn't! And PLEASE stop calling me 'Vic'!"

Wow. Pat is REALLY short compared to the Cybercontroller.

Oh neat, we actually got a connecting plot point to the events of The Moonbase.

Grabby Cyberman are grabby, and only Jamie escapes!

Whoops, now he's been zapped. And...I just realized: how exactly are his legs not freezing? I mean, he's got knee-socks but...that kilt.

Usually I don't approve of exaggerated or pointless-ish companion screaming, but sometimes they make excellent distractions.

Hatch is open! RESCUE TIME.

Jamie McCrimmon pawing at someone other than the Doctor? For shame!

Cling-counter: 4

Wow, the Cybermen seem to be particularly abusive of Toberman, don't they?

So now everyone's out except Klieg and Toberman and, aww Jamie got to save Victoria when whacking the Cyberman with the thermos didn't work.

Moar cybermats! And...guys, I really don't think we needed that close-up of multiple cyber-ass.

The first time I watched this I was pretty creeped out by the cybermats, but now they're actually kinda cute.

WAIT. OH MY GOD. THIS SCENE. And I forgot that it opened with such nice music.

I would quote this whole scene if I could, but instead I'll just do That Speech that stabs everyone in the d'awwww place.

"You probably can't remember your family."
"Oh yes I can when I want to, and that's the point, really. I have to really *want* to to bring them back in front of my eyes. The rest

of the time they...they sleep in my mind, and I forget, and so will you. Oh yes you will! You'll find there's so much else to think about, to remember. Our lives are different to anybody else's. That's the exciting thing, because nobody in the universe can do what we're doing. You must get some sleep, and let this poor old man stay awake."

...Patrick Troughton, I would listen to you read the dictionary that was so beautiful.

I'm not sure what surprises me more: the fact that nobody heard the cybermats coming, or that Two is holding a gun.

Victoria was able to blast one earlier so...WHY can't she just tell the others to shoot them now? ...oh wait, the plot.

Ah, so THAT was the thing they were talking about on Tumblr where Pat started to say "Frazer" instead of "Jamie."

Partially-converted cyber-Toberman! And...the Cybermen are getting back in their pods?

Considering all the .gifs I've seen of that head-pat, it was surprisingly quick. Seriously, like...less than a second. Oh well...

Cling-counter: 5

They're actually helping the Cybercontroller into the machine...cling-counter: 6

And now he's trapped! Cling-counter: 7

"If the Cyberman is aroused, we shall be ready for him." #doubleentendresididntneedtoheartoday

lol cardboard

Dead bitch is dead.

And suddenly, Toberman was a serious frigging badass. Time to THROW SOME CYBERMANS.

Huh. If you look closely when Jamie's pushing the dead Cyberman down the hatch, you'll see it's pushing itself down a little.

Aww, Toberman doesn't want to leave his dead mistress. Also, there's a LOT of villains pretending to be asleep in this serial, aren't there?

Oh Jamie, you go down to check on Two and then you get captured. *sigh*

"Precisely...yes...Master of the World!"
"Well now I KNOW you're mad. I just wanted to make sure."

And then Klieg got Cyberman'd. Cling-counter: 8

Ewww...cyber-pus. Cling-counter: 9

"Last time, they were frozen for five centuries. This time, it must be forever!" Oh. You. Just. Wait.

And Jamie trips on the stairs...cling-counter: 10

"When I say 'run'...run." Two and Jamie vs. Cybercontroller. WHO SHALL WIN?

And Toberman goes out with a good solid heroic sacrifice. Good on you, mate.

A single cybermat escapes, leaving the door open for the next cyber-attack. That would be...The Wheel in Space, right?

Originally Posted October 26ᵗʰ, 2010

THE ABOMINABLE SNOWMEN

Written by Mervyn Haisman and Henry Lincoln
Aired: September 30 – November 4, 1967

And after horror and lots of man-screaming, we return to the TARDIS with our heroes fresh from the Tomb 'o Cybermans.

Also Two sounds really REALLY excited to be here. (just as I'm realizing that the setting reminds me how behind I am on my Buddhism reading)

"Well, em...whatever it is, it's nice to see it again." Oh Doctor, you big magpie you... #butseriouslywhatisthatthing #itlooksnicethough

JAMIE HAS DISCOVERED BAGPIPES. JAMIE HAS DISCOVERED BAGPIPES. JAMIE HAS DISCOVERED BAGPIPES. JAMIE HAS DISCOVERED BAGPIPES.

"Hey, I could fix those easily!"
"Yes, I was afraid of that."

Ah yes, Two's epic fur coat. And according to Victoria, he looks "beautiful" in it. #patricktroughtonwasaveryprettygirl

"Oh, don't ask me. When you've been with the Doctor as long as I have, you begin t' realize you don't know WHAT he's talking about."

The big hairy beastie is the Doctor. The big hairy beastie is the Doctor.

Once again reminded how epic Pat's teeth are.

Two's being strangely secretive and scatterbrained. He really does seem to know something right off the bat that we don't about this place.

YETI FEET. YETI FEET. YETI FEET.

"Come on, it's a marvelous view!" Actually, it looks a lot like the quarry from last time, except colder.

Even with his jailbait socks all the way up (don't ask, not my idea), Jamie is still cold. #downsidesofkilts

Also, aww, he's such a good big-brother figure to Victoria.

"Wait while I get that sword."
("They disappear into the TARDIS where Jamie equips himself with winter coat and weapon.")
BEAR COUNTRY.

And of COURSE they just happen to land near a murder site and get blamed for it.

Interesting how Jamie's and Victoria's attitudes towards chasing the "beastie" flip completely when they see the cave might be manmade.

Awww, cling.
"If you need me, just yell your head off."
"Don't worry, I will!"

Yikes. Travers is one paranoid chap, isn't he.

Just a guess, but what's the betting that the dude with the facial hair is really a bad guy? #beardofevil

YETIIIIIIIIIII!!!

Now all I have to do is make it through the rest of this serial without saying "balls are touching"......dammit.

"Och, don't worry about that. It's quite dead." OR IS IT?
#DUNDUNDUUUUN

Good tactic: try talking to the one person in the monastery who
seems like a "reasonable chap" even though you've just met him.

So it sounds like the Doctor's been here before and...stole something
important from them?

Although considering how frantically he was looking for it earlier, I'm
assuming he took it by mistake or something.

I THINK THIS MIGHT BE THE MOST ADORABLE CHASE
SCENE EVER.

Abbot, what is even on your head.

Oh. Hello, Mysterious Unseen Voice.

Sad-Two does not approve of bondage.

So I wonder if the Mysterious Unseen Voice here is the Great
Intelligence that I hear about every once in a while with this story.

Oh Jamie, making up for lost cling time, are we? Also, why is
everyone screaming about the Yeti when we haven't seen any in this
scene yet?

Ah yes, and there's Two's well-I-did-tell-you-so face.

Also, the Mysterious Unseen Voice has suddenly turned evil-
sounding. Gee, I wonder what that could possibly imply.

TRIO OF YETI!!! (in case you haven't noticed yet, I REALLY like
the Yeti)

"If they do, do you think you could capture one? I would like to
examine one!"
"Examine it? Aye we'll wrap it up for ye!"
"Thank you Jamie!"

Aaaaand why exactly was Two so afraid of Jamie "having an idea?"

OH GOD YOU CAN HEAR THE THUMPING OF
THE MONKS HITTING THE YETI OH GOD NO D':
#ireallyreallywanttohugayeti

There were literally tears in my eyes for a few seconds just now.

Retreating Yeti, and when did Jamie get a wristwatch.

Well that explains why the Yeti stopped: it lost its sphere. But now
the sphere is moving o_o

And they're calling to each other...how are they even movin...oh wait,
I can actually see little wheels on them.

Wait...HOW exactly do you reason that mechanical Yeti automatically
mean that there are real Yeti up there? They could all be mechanical.

Ah yes, the routine asking the guards where you put your balls.
#reallystupidjokes

This is the second Second Doctor story I've seen that has someone
in it called "the master" who isn't really the Master.

So this whole thing is being operated by a Yeti chessboard? Well okay
then.

BALL-RETRIEVAL.

Oh hey look, the monks have a segment of the Key to Time.

Okay. I think I've officially lost track of who's under trance when to
do what and who isn't. #stupidmindcontrol

Thankfully, suspicious Victoria is suspicious.

Um, yeah, somehow I don't think an incense burner is going to stop
a Yeti. Unless it likes pretty smells.

Or you could just show it to the door, that works too.

"Have you thought up some clever plan, Doctor?"

"Yes, Jamie, I believe I have."

"What are you going to do?"

"Bung a rock at it."

Emasculate the robot Yeti #bytakingawayitsballs #ohgodhannahshutupthatjokeisdead

"It's sending out a signal! Just as we wanted." Two's creeperface. Not exactly as we wanted.

"It disappeared 300 years ago."

"Oh, stolen?"

"No, it was given to a stranger for...safe keeping during a time of trouble."

And now we know.

Although we still don't know exactly what the trouble was...

NOW the monks are finally getting suspicious of their leader.

Oh wow. Two told Jamie "no heroics" and Jamie actually listened to him. Impressive show of willpower there.

Oh WOW. Victoria just FAKED A POISONING to trick her friend and escape a cell. I must admit, that's s a new one.

(okay, so technically it's a ploy I've seen before, but not like that)

So I know that Victoria was trying to escape, but I'm not that clear on what she hopes to accomplish by this point, other than finding Two.

Oh. OH. THAT'S WHAT THE GUY LOOKS LIKE. Not gonna lie: CREEPY.

("The veils around the ancient Tibetan have lifted.") ...but how are we so sure he's Tibetan? He seems pretty alien to me.

Unless, of course, he's being controlled by a higher alien power or something like that.

Oh fun, more companion hypnosis.

So I just remembered that the "pyramid" that Travers keeps talking about could be mistaken for the pyramid of Yeti spheres in the cave.

Geez, EVERYBODY'S mind's getting scrambled in this story.

Yeti SMASH.

WOAH. Monk crushed by a toppling Buddha statue. Not something I was expecting to see today.

It's all fun and games until the big cuddly monsters KILL A GUY WITH A RELIGIOUS ICON.

Yup, the Tibetan guy does appear to be speaking to some Higher Alien Power.

"I have chosen to speak to you myself through the lips of this maiden." ...I'm actually kinda glad this part is missing because CREEPY.

To clarify: Victoria. Speaking in a man-voice.

Oh. Well at least he's courteous enough to prove Team Two's innocence in these shenanigans.

"THERE you are, I've been worried sick! Where've you been?" Jamie McCrimmon: Scottish piper, human clingwrap, mother hen.

Well, at least the monks know that Victoria's in a trance.

Okay, maybe NOW we'll get an explanation for what the Doctor's history with this place is.

"Good to look upon your face again..." So I'm assuming this means he's met Two before, but when? Considering Jamie's presence, the only logical timeslot would be immediately between Power of the Daleks and The Highlanders.

And there's Pat's Kindly Old Uncle voice. Love that voice, and he does it so damn WELL. Not sure any other Doctor could quite pull that off.

Well, it looks like the old man's finally been released to the peace of death after 300 years.

OH WAIT. NO HE HASN'T. AND HE MIGHT BE EVIL-ER NOW.

Interesting contrast of priorities: Jamie's immediate concern is Victoria while Two is focusing on the greater scheme at hand.

Holy crap. You know what this kinda reminds me of? The Fires of Pompeii. Think about it...

Ten was worried about not breaking the timeline, but Donna wanted to save just one family. Doctor: Big picture. Companion: Little picture.

Actually, I'll bet if I thought about this long enough, I'd see that pattern with most Doctor-companion relationships.

Ah, sure enough, Jamie talks Two into taking care of Victoria first.

"Sleep...sleep...sleep...oh not you, Jamie."
"Hey WHAT? O_O"
AHAHAHA oh Jamie I love you. #hisFACE

"Hey, I never knew you could do that sort of thing!" Jamie, Patrick Troughton is basically his own hypnotic device. He's just that awesome.

REVELATIONS. SOME PANICKING. ALL IN TIME FOR A CLIFFHANGER.

Incandescent masses pouring from the mouths of caves usually aren't a good sign.

Huh. I guess the mustachioed guy I pegged as a villain earlier really isn't such a bad guy after all. And now it looks like he's going to die.

Yup, he's dead. Poor guy. And now Two has to contend with Disembodied Evil Laughter.

The problem with escaping from evil: you have to locate it first.

Is it just me, or is Victoria getting sidelined quite a bit in this story?

Another one of those times where I to wonder if hypnosis is just a general Doctor-power. Actually, it might be a general Time Lord-power.

Time for another game of Yeti Chess!

One party goes smashing, another gets to pray. Guess which ones Victoria and Jamie are put in.

"Who are you?"
"You know well, it is I: the Master."
Except it really isn't, although he'd probably call himself the Great Intelligence too.

Two DEFIES your attempts to prove your God Mode!

Ack. No, seriously, what is your face.
This shall not be settled with swords or guns or even wits, but with CREEPER FACES.

Kind of a shame they had to set up that whole scene only to have it used once and just for the sake of being destroyed.

Oh. Turns out that prayer thing from earlier might help Victoria help to save the day.

"JAAAAMIIIIIE! YEEEETI COMIIIING!" ...why exactly did you need to be pulling your face for that?

(when I say pulling his face, I don't mean the regular kind of pulling a face, I mean PULLING his FACE.)

And it all boiled down to Jamie breaking balls.
#ineverlearnwhenajokeisdead

Oh wait. Never mind. There's still craziness going around here.

That's more than just a s'plosion. That's a volcanic eruption. Or in this case, an intellectual eruption.

And so they say goodbye to the monastery and depart for adventures through time and space once more.

"A Yeti! A REAL Yeti! At last!" Aww, and it even makes frightened growling sounds!

"Just lookit my knees, they're bright blue!" Well Jamie, maybe you should roll your socks up a little higher. #tumblrinjoke

Also, it doesn't sound like your next adventure is going to land you anyplace warmer.

Originally Posted February 8th, 2011

THE ICE WARRIORS

Written by Brian Davis
Aired: November 11 – December 16, 1967

Hello, Control Room Full of People in Zebra Suits! And what's that weird voice-over that sounds like a dying Dalek?

But seriously, I can barely understand a word that thing's saying.

I can only assume that the odd fashion choices were yet another victim of the 60s. But SO MUCH WHITE. EVERYWHERE.

Ice Warrior helmet! Wow, from here that thing actually does look pretty creepy. Big blank eye sockets...

The TARDIS just materialized on its SIDE. With the top angled DOWNWARD. And it SLID. I don't think we've ever seen this before. o_O

"OWW!"
"What's the matter?"
"YOU'RE ON MY HEAD!"
fall
Well, that explains what Two was standing on. Poor Jamie's head.

Wait. Now all three of them are up and I STILL DON'T KNOW WHAT THEY'RE STANDING ON. The console isn't that close to the door, is it?

Jamie's knee on Two's hand. Revenge for earlier, but I don't think Two will be in a very clingy mood after this.

Aww, Victoria is such a pretty snow princess in that cloak. I wonder if Jamie actually has anything on his legs this time.

Answer: not really. Except his socks. And you know when he's down to just his socks what time it is. IT'S BUSINESS...IT'S BUSINESS TI-*gack*

That was another installment of Hannah Making References to Shows She Hasn't Actually Seen. #flightoftheconchords

Also, it is just me, or does every TV show ever have exactly the same wolf/coyote howl effect?

"There's something wrong with its pitch."
"Oh no. Now look, it might be dangerous. Now let's LEAVE it."
"No!"
"Doctor..."
"Let's go in."

And who could say no to that voice? :D

PEOPLE. LISTEN TO THE COSMIC HOBO IN THE GIANT COAT. HE KNOWS WHAT HE'S TALKING ABOUT.

"Warriors of the ice...who stood over seven feet tall...DOCTOR IN DISTRESS..."

So I'm assuming these two bearded guys in the big fur coats are real scavengers. Weren't they stealing food from the base earlier?

AVALAAAAAAAANCHE.

Oh wait, the guy with the stubble was the one they were talking about earlier who was presumably exiled from the base for some reason.

This story is making me wonder: exactly how many Earth's Future scenarios has this show thrown our way over the years?

Agh, having American ears, it's really weird hearing "glaciers" pronounced "GLASS-ee-ers" every ten seconds instead of "GLAY-shers."

"Now you wait here and don't touch anything!" But they're certainly allowed to Cling.

"Ah, Victoria, did you see how those lassies were dressed?"
"Yes I did, and trust YOU to think of something like THAT!"
"Oh I...I couldn't help thinkin' about it!"
"Well I think it's disgusting, wearing that kind of...thing!"
"Oh, so it is, so it is! You...you don't see yourself dressed like that then?"
"JAMIE!"
"Oh I'm sorry it was just an idea."
"We will now change the subject please."

The Ice Warrior awakens! And he looks pretty grumpy, too.

Barely a minute and a half into the episode and everybody's already unconscious.

Oh wait, Jamie's up and about again. Mini info-dump time, and of COURSE Victoria's been kidnapped.

Good ol' Jamie, always the first to make all the science people stop technobabbling and Save The Girl.

Ah, first time in over a year I've heard the Ice Warrior's voices. Still not that fond of them.

So it SOUNDS like the Ice Warrior wants to find its crewmates and leave in peace, which of course means that SOMETHING is going to go wrong.

So he isn't sure whether they want to go back or conquer Earth. NOW we know.

"Victoria's important too, ye know!"
"You don't seem to realize, boy, the whole fate of the world could be at stake!"

I'm not gonna lie, I was totally expecting a "your girlfriend isn't more important than the whole universe - SHE IS TO ME!" moment.

Wait, what does that guy mean by "flat on his back for weeks?" That avalanche only happened maybe a couple hours ago.

"I'm going for drugs, but if I don't get them you're as good as dead."
...? What is this "context" that you speak of?

"What is that??"
"Sonic gun. It'll burst you brain with noisssssssssse."
Ah yes, forgot about the Ice Warriors' snake-like hissing thing.

"I trust no one, Doctor. Not anymore. Human emotions are...unreliable."
sad Troughton-face :(

This is going to sound like a really really strange observation during this scene but...that Ice Warrior has quite unusual buttocks.

(I won't be surprised if I'm the first American since Forrest Gump to say "buttocks")

"Well, he's a scientist and he's a bit inclined to have his head in the air. You know what they're like!"
"Aye, I certainly do."
#JAMIIIEEEE

Hello, what's this? The head scientist is actually showing a bit of concern for another person? Hell really HAS frozen over.

"This is a formal establishment and our regulations..."
"Oh, regulations do not apply to me. I work in my own way, freely."
Tell 'im, Two.

Wait, the woman from the base found her way to the plant museum, but she doesn't seem to be wearing protective gear. Are they connected?

Maybe it's just me, but this is turning out to be one of those more talkative serials. And it's still a recon episode.

Oh wait, I take that back. Someone's being threatened with a gun now.

Actually, have they explained yet what that bearded Scottish guy's deal is?

Uh oh, we've got a small troop of Ice Warriors on our hands. And Victoria's valiant attempts to reason with them are failing miserably.

Oo, um, hey, uh...you've got something under your nose.

Back to Two in the work room and suddenly FAST MUSIC.

Also, he sounds HORRIBLY sleep-deprived. Someone get this man some coffee.

"Omega...now what does he mean...Omega..." After seeing The Three Doctors all those months ago, that's all I can think of.

Aww, Two has his big breakthrough and then someone else is all "DENIED."

Looks like the Ice Warriors have found their ship. It's probably just the shadows, but from here it looks like a giant bunch of grapes.

OI. ICE WARRIORS. GTFO OF JAMIE. BAD MARTIANS. BAD.

Lying on the ground like that, Jamie almost looks like he's wearing shorts.

("Jamie, partially shielded by Arden's body, is still alive.") YAAAAY! Hurray for meat shields!

"Somewhere out on that ice face are two young people for whom I have considerable affection!" Awwwwwwww...

Having another moment where I wouldn't mind having Polly around to mother Jamie.

Come to think of it, I'd like to be there mothering him right about now too. Poor lamb, all a wreck and he just wants to save his girl.

("Victoria, meanwhile, has managed to escape from her captors.")
...Wow. When did THIS happen?

Oh. Maybe the Ice Warriors know about this already. OH RIGHT.
She's bait. Of course.

Oh my god. Two's face. When he's trying to find out about Jamie. My
heart. It is break.

And now we're out of recon territory and back to the Land of the
Moving.

Two shakes his head in disapproval of these shenanigans as Clent
tries to get a grieving Victorian girl to describe rocket engines to him.

So now I'm wondering how much of the Ice Warriors' faces are
prosthetics and how much isn't. I'd thought the mouths were natural,
but...

Need a chemical? Just dial it on the rotary phone! (No really, that's
what they're doing.)

"Yes, there's something I need rather desperately." *dials* *vial
drops*
"Well, what's that?"
"Water." *glug*

The Doctor: off to take on fully-armed hostile aliens with just a coat,
his wits, and a vial of ammonium sulfate. #science

Victoria, that was way too deliberate a scream for someone trying to
hide. Making an avalanche? Making an echo? Or just luring it off?

Aaaaand now she's dropped the communicator. How that Ice Warrior
hasn't spotted her black cloak against the ice yet, I have no idea.

Wow. Multi-purpose avalanche. It's also a scene transition!

Oh goodness, Jamie is like a cornered cat. Kitty wants OUT. Kitty
doesn't WANT to take his medicine. Kitty will BITE you.

"I'm a loyalist!"

"A loyalist!"

Maybe Kitty's made a new friend! (Someone please stop me from calling Jamie "Kitty" for the whole story.)

"But what is it, then?"

"Well their weapons must have affected your central nervous system."

"You mean I'm paralyzed?"

NONONONONONONONONONO

NONONONONONONONONONONONONONONONONON-
ONONO

NONONONO

(okay, stopping there because I know he'll be alright, but the idea of Jamie thinking he'll never walk again is not good for my happy)

Huh. With all those circles on the walls, the Ice Warrior ship almost looks like the TARDIS interior.

Seriously, the Ice Warriors are like giant turtles. They could very easily slip their heads inside their big bulky shell-like bodies.

...oh. I've seen this screencap of Jamie sprawled out like that with the caption "draw me like one of your French girls" soooo many times.

Of course, now that I actually know the context, it's quite a bit less Terrible and more terrible. #tumblrinjokes

Ah, looks like Victoria's going to get rescued by the hairy Scottish guy. Maybe he can reunite her with Jamie!

Hello again, Two! Found the Ice Warriors' ship yet?

Why do I have an uncomfortable feeling that Storr is going to be the Well-Intentioned Extremist who sides with the bad guys?

Ugh. I can't stop thinking about how the Ice Warriors have probably my least favorite monster design in the history of Doctor Who.

I apologize to everyone who likes them, but...I'm sorry, I really don't care for them very much.

However, I AM grateful that their sonic guns don't have the same wobbly effect here that they did in The Seeds of Death.

WHEW. Two sounds really confident about Jamie's recovery. Athough he hasn't really explained how. Just "a matter of time."

TWO. PLEASE GET YOUR FACE AWAY FROM THE GIANT GUN STICKING OUT OF THE DOOR.

Also, please answer the Ice Warrior's question before you literally explode.

"One...two...three..."
"Oh, alright, alright!"
...wow. That defused the cliffhanger pretty efficiently.

"That's very civil of you oh my word..." Ahn ahn, sorry Two, it's too late to leave now.

Victoria! Hug times now!

There's those wolves again, and this time we actually see their paw prints. Maybe they're actually going to be plot-relevant soon?

Yup. The last stretch through open country back to the base. And Jamie still can't walk. I sense an impending miraculous recovery.

OH WAIT. THAT'S NOT A WOLF. THAT'S A BEAR. THEY SAID WOLVES. BUT I'M PRETTY SURE THAT'S A BEAR.

Ah, clever Two, hiding the communicator in his massive epic coat and sneaking instructions to the base.

I still can't understand about 70% of that frigging computer voice.

YES THAT IS TOTALLY A BEAR AND THE TRANQ GUN ISN'T WORKING ON IT AND IT'S GETTING CLOSER AND THEN CUTAWAY

Uh oh, it sounds like Mrs. Garrett is almost about to lose her cool about this. #honestlynopunintended

Oh. I guess the tranquilizer gun kicked in after all. Run from sleeping bear!

Classic classic scene. The baddies are demanding information "OR THE GIRL DIES." Cue "DON'T TELL THEM!" and the hero giving in anyway.

"You won't succeed! You CAN'T be so inhuman!" Victoria, while I admire your faith in other races, they're from MARS.

Nice glass hat. What exactly is that for? Is that an interface? No that can't be it, you've talked to the computer without it before...

Oh my god. Jamie's face when he's told that the Doctor and Victoria are going to be left to die...

Dramatic escalation of tensions and then MORE TRANQUILIZING!

So are we ever going to find out specifically what happened between Clent and Penley? Or is that being left to subtext and overtones?

Oh Two, that's so improper of you! Making a lady cry! (diversion diversion diversion SCIENCE)

You know, that's probably the best subversion of "the bad guys are just a few feet away, we can just stage-whisper" I've seen on this show.

Aaaaaaaand Two can't get the vial open! This is not a good thing! MORE DIVERSIONS!

WAIT WHY DON'T YOU JUST THROW IT ON THE GROUND AND SMASH IT OR SOMETHING IT MIGHT BE YOUR ONLY OPTION NOW

Attagirl, Victoria! But wait, why was Two trying to get the dying Warrior's hand onto that control panel?

This is interestingly anachronistic: the base's computer room, with all its nice shiny future white-ness, has a chandelier on the ceiling.

And finally somebody stands up and calls out the computer as a load of bull. So, naturally, he gets shot.

Well, at least Clent is making a solid effort at diplomacy. Now if it wasn't for That One Dude on the Floor With the Gun...

This is probably just me failing utterly at science, but couldn't they just MAKE the mercury they need from that chemical synthesizer?

"What are your qualifications for existenccccce?" Woah. That's... that's actually pretty deep.

Something I've noticed about Clent: he walks around with a cane, but it's never explained or integrated into his character.

I mean, One carried a cane sometimes, but that was just for show. Clent actually *needs* it to walk right.

Two, creatures with "much greater fluid contents" than human beings would have to be a metric crapton of water.

"There is just a vague risk that it will kill everybody." Ahhhhh ha. Good to know, I guess.

Oh. Well, thank you, camera. Thank you for opening with a shot that could easily be angled up Jamie's kilt. #TerriblePeopleClub

So all Penley had to do was crank up the heat? Maybe Two doesn't need to launch his possible-death-ray after all.

On the other hand, we've reached the only-10-minutes-left-still-room-for-one-more-thing-to-go-wrong point in the story.

And there goes the gun after all. JESUS Clent sounds like he's in a ton of pain o_O

Ah, looks like Jamie's up and about again JAMIE'S UP AND

ABOUT AGAIN HE CAN WALK IT'S A PLOT-CONVENIENT MIRACLE!

insert "I'M MEEEEEELTING" joke here

"Penley, you are the most...insufferably...irritating and...infuriating... person...I've ever...been privileged...to work with."
"Thank you."

Wait...did Victoria somehow put the TARDIS right-side-up while all that was going on? Because it's standing up again.

Also, this is the first time I've seen the top of the end credits hovering at the bottom of the screen while waiting for the music to start.

Originally Posted March 24th, 2011

THE ENEMY OF THE WORLD

Written by David Whitaker
Aired: December 23, 1967 – January 27, 1968

Oh goodness, the TARDIS sounds ill today. Also, VICTORIA. MY MY WHAT A SHORT SKIRT YOU'RE WEARING.

(Short, as in Two can't use Jamie as a defense anymore.)

Aww, he's brought them to the beach for a little seaside vacation! How thoughtful. *counts minutes before things go horribly wrong*

("The Doctor meanwhile has stripped to his longjohns and is merrily crashing about in the surf.") Probably the only moment of Two stripping.

Ah, you must be Astrid! There are some characters here I've heard about so many times it feels like I know them already...

hits stopwatch Three minutes: people are already aiming guns at the Doctor.

So we already have burninated: wet, half-naked Doctor and a hovercraft chase scene with guns. And we're only 5 minutes in. *glares*

"Perhaps we've landed in a world of madmen!"
"They're human beings, if that's what you mean. Indulging their favorite pastime: trying to destroy each other."

89

Wow. One thing's for sure: the soundtrack people were certainly having a lot of fun with this.

("In the cockpit, Victoria clings to Jamie for dear life.") CANON-CLING.

"But what is this thing, Doctor!"
"It's a helicopter, Jamie!"
"Huh?"
"A chopper! You know, a whirlybird!"
"...He says it's a bird!"

I still don't understand why the Doctor keeps saying he's not a doctor of medicine when he clearly has a good amount of medical expertise.

Oh wow. Two gets one great compliment and suddenly he's a puppy at Astrid's feet. *scratches his ears*

"You resemble, very closely, a man who's determined to become dictator of the world. A man who will stop at nothing." SALAMANDERRRR

Sorry, I probably should've saved that until he actually showed up.

And then there was a s'plosion! That helicopter was so nice and patient for waiting until there were antagonistic men with guns on board.

Ooo yay, history lesson! Because it isn't a future-Earth Classic Who story without a history lesson.

So apparently the United Nations is the United Zones now.

Theeeeeeere he is, the man himself. And good god, with just the audio and telesnaps it's hard to take him seriously at all with THAT ACCENT.

"He seems to be a public benefactor, quite a speaker too and remarkably handsome, didn't you think so Jamie?" Jamie thinks you look gorgeous

Now this is interesting: I honestly wasn't expecting Salamander to be introduced as a positive public figure (with dark secrets, of course).

So let's see how much of a chameleon Two can be. He has as many minutes to more or less *become* Salamander.

Aaaaaand it looks like he's about done it!

Patrick Troughton is brilliant beyond everything. He plays Salamander and Twomander similarly but still VERY distinctly.

And the best part, you can tell even with just the audio and stills. THAT, my dear followers, is some Serious Business acting talent.

You can still hear him trying to master the accent and everything oh my god

Now this is interesting: for once, Team TARDIS seems daunted by the prospect of saving the world. That's every day for them, isn't it?

BENIK! Someone else I feel like I know already because I've heard so much about you!

Ohhhh man, SO many awkward creepy close-ups of angry!Bruce in this episode...

SALAMANDEEEEERRRRRRR We meet at last!

And he's talking about volcanoes. I think I know where this is going.

Fariah! I know you too!

Ohhhhh my goodness, Jamie's sweatervest. How did I not notice that until now.

"Spot trouble"? I wonder if this is what they envisioned cellular telephones being like at this point in the future.

DEFUSED YETI. DEFUSED YETI. DISUSED JETTY.

Sorry, it WAS "disused Yeti" that Two misheard. But still, DEFUSED YETI.

Wait. Is it just me, or does Fariah have Princess Leia buns in her hair?

And she had "help" with her food-tasting duties...ahaaaaa, I knew there was something suspicious about that wine.

Suddenly, ACTION-JAMIE!

This interaction between Jamie and Salamander is blowing my mind a bit. Pat, you are a serious SERIOUS chameleon.

Also, I honestly have to wonder if Jamie means "girlfriend" as in "romantic interest" or "friend who is a girl."

"What an extraordinary young man!"
"I prize loyalty very highly, my friend, and I repay it very generously."
And very naively.

I mean, I'm honestly not sure how I'd react to some random dude coming up to me and claiming to've saved my life.

So we've got two of the three main female characters in this serial working the kitchens. Not sure how I feel about this.

On the other hand, Fariah is doing a great job of saving herself from utter racefail by being intelligent, cunning, and even a bit badass.

Ooohhhhh Salamander, you sly devious bastard.

And now all the jokes that the TPC make about him playing with volcanoes make sense.

Amused a bit that they credit Patrick Troughton as Dr. Who Salamander.

Huh. Now that I can actually see Salamander moving, I can see a lot more Troughton in him.

Correction: a LOT lot more Troughton. Even hearing the accent sounds different now.

On another note, Jamie continues to be awesome and badass and now as an added bonus he's leatherclad.

And now that I can see Victoria properly, I see Jamie's rubbing off on her more: she's started wearing tartan kilts now.

Awwww, she's so happy remembering her pudding.

Another great moment of Jamie is Smarter Than He Looks: he certainly understands the methods of tyrants and political puppets.

"A sort of Jekyll and Hyde character, our Mr. Salamander." Same could be said here in general: Good Trought, Evil Trought.

"SECURITY! QUICK!" *shoves Two into a box*
"I hope there's plenty of air in here!"

Ah, Benik! Fancy running into you again.

So you can't force a man to leave his home outside the boundaries, but you *can* smash the everloving crap out of his stuff.

JEEEEEEEEESUS Benik is a massive slimeball. MAAAAAAASSIVE slimeball. Grrrrrrrrrrrr...

"People spend all their time making nice things and then other people come along and break them."

Two does not look to be taking kindly to your screaming nearly in his ear.

Wow. The Russian-sounding guard gets one look at Astrid unzipping her jacket to get her pass and he's already asking her out for wine.

Um...Astrid...I think you can zip your jacket up again now.

"How's the food? *sniff* Terrible, terrible. I'll get the sack tonight, I swear I will! Maybe they'll shoot me and I won't have to worry anymore. Nah, they wouldn't do that. The firing squad'd miss me." I really like this cook.

Yikes. Fariah's still got quite a bite. I wonder if we'll ever find out how she wound up with Salamander...

Uh oh, somebody's getting their food poisoned.

Or maybe not! Looks like the cowardly guy's still got a solid conscience after all.

Aaaaaaand now he's dead, thanks to poisoned wine. This really shouldn't surprise me.

Correction: I REALLY like this cook. Funny guy.

Well, that rescue plan failed.

Uh oh, Salamander's got his first hint of his doppelganger.

Ah, Pat's credited as Dr. Who Salamander here too, except with slightly more space so it looks more like two separate names.

Ah yes, the infamous Land of No Telesnaps.

"Why should you want to help him?"
"Because I hate Salamander probably even more than you do. I can help you destroy him!"
BAMF!Fariah.

Also, Benik really loves rolling her name around in his mouth, doesn't he?

So, um, no reaction from Fariah to seeing her boss's double? Or was she told already and I just forgot?

"What you really want me to do is to kill him, isn't it?"
"What *else* do you do when someone is evil?"
Ahhhha. Two, explain.

Escaping through the ventilation shaft, that works too...

BENIK IS A SHOUTY MAN.

Ohhhhhh crap. Fariah's going to die before we learn anything more about her (FROM her, anyway) D:

"You can't threaten me now, Benik. I can only die once. And someone's beaten you to it."

"Who was the other man?"

"Sir! She's dead."

"...Good."

And so falls An Awesome Woman.

Wait...what's Salamander doing now? I hope he finishes up soon because that buzzer sound is REALLY REALLY ANNOYING.

There we go. Also, I really wish this scene had proper telesnaps. The situation was just odd enough to really merit a specific visual aid.

Hello, who are these random underground refugee people?

It sounds like these are people that he's deliberately keeping underground under the impression that the surface is uninhabitable. But why?

Salamander's even faking radiation sickness. This is an odd plot thread to be introducing so late-ish in the serial.

So they've been down there for nearly 5 years? I suddenly feel like I'm watching a completely different serial.

This plot is even complete with a Rebellious Youth Who Doesn't Believe The Lies and His Lady Friend. Wow.

Aaaaaand now we've cut back to Two in full Salamander get-up! I remember what I'm watching now.

Ah, tracking device. Of course. So Salamander's man knows about Two now.

Wow. Astrid sure had an easy time swiping that gun. Are all the local women in this serial just really badass by default?

Two says he doesn't want any part of violence, but a few seconds later he asks for the gun. ...Well okay then.

Ahhhhh, I see what you did there. Now they've actually got Bruce on their side, to an extent.

Seeds of doubt cast in the mind of the Faithful Underground Elder thanks to the magic of newspaper dating!

"You've LIED to us, haven't you?" Ohhhh snap.

Wait. Wait...Wait. What does he mean by "the natural disasters WE'VE been organizing?" HOW HAVE THEY BEEN CAUSING EARTHQUAKES/VOLCANOES.

Not sure if Salamander's doing the best job of covering his tracks. He keeps making basically the same argument over and over again.

"Promise me one thing: you won't tell the others."
"Why shouldn't I?"
"BECAUSE I AM RIGHT AND YOU ARE WRONG!"
#EVILTROUGHT

Aw, poor frustrated angsty Colin.

Jamie and Victoria are finally up! Feels like we haven't seen them in a while.

"Come now, you don't think I'm just going to sit here and ask questions, do you?"
"You must've been a nasty little boy."
"Oh, I was!"

BENIIIIIIK. GREASY SLIMEBAAAAAAAALL.

"You lay a finger on her, I'll kill you." This is a James Robert McCrimmon Appreciation Post.

Suddenly, TWOMANDER! Wow. He's certainly nailing the accent this time.

Wait. Unless that's really Salamander. I am confuse. But it's probably Two because he mentioned the Doctor.

"Fariah is dead."
"DEAD?"
"You've had her murdered too, have you?"

"WHY YOU..."
"NO, VICTORIA, DON'T HIT ME! You wouldn't hit your old friend the Doctor, would you? I wouldn't leave you in the tender mercy of Salamander!"
"...Doctor?"
"You don't believe me? Oh..."
("He pats his pockets hopefully, before realizing that he is not carrying his recorder.")
DDD:

Saved by the Power of Music! Happy reunion! Awwww...

Confused Benik is confused.

Huh. Well, I guess now we know what happened to all those people that allegedly went with Salamander to the surface and never came back.

And I guess Swann escaped after all to be rescued by Astrid! But it sounds like he's a total wreck.

Oh sure, give the man some random water dripping down a cave wall. I'm sure THAT'S safe. (Well, okay he might be dying, but still.)

Sneaky Benik and equally sneaky Two. Who's going to crack first?

And now Swann is dead. At least he got all the important information to Astrid in his final moments.

"Tell him where I am and just say 'redhead'."
"Redhead."
"Redhead. Is that clear?"
"Redhead...is that your wife?"
#jamiiiieeeee

Astrid finds the refugees and is immediately pelted by stuff from angry frightened people. Lovely. Ah thank you for the intervention, Colin.

So the Geiger counter was a set-up after all! And how does Astrid prove it? With a simple desk ruler. Nice.

You know, I didn't notice it until just now but...is it just me, or does Kent have an American accent?

Wait. WAIT. The Salamander Kent is talking to is actually Two? But... when did he get in the records room?

AND SUDDENLY EVERYTHING IS HAPPENING AT ONCE. Oh wow. Trought's got an EVIL laugh.

S'PLOSION! And Kent and Salamander are dead. Ne'er the twins shall meet.

OH. WAIT. NEVER MIND. THERE THEY BOTH ARE.

"We're going to put you outside, Salamander. No friends, no safety, nothing. You'll run, but they'll catch up with you."
"NO!"

("In a flash, Salamander has the Doctor pinned against the console.") WAIT. WHAT. AND WE CAN'T SEE THIS BECAUSE BURNINATORS.

Thrown out into the Time Vortex...wow, what a way to die.

Originally Posted April 10th, 2011

THE WEB OF FEAR

Written by Mervyn Haisman and Henry Lincoln
Aired: February 3 – March 9, 1968

Oh wow. Oh WOW. I know your budget was microscopic but... replacing the actual roundels with full-length photos in the middle of the wall?

Also, does anyone else find it odd that the TARDIS just *happens* to be tilting in the direction of the open doors?

But I digress. CLING!

"I wonder..." More importantly, YETIIIIII!

Wait a sec...is this the same explorer guy from The Abominable Snowmen? *checks* It is! Professor Travers! And played by Jack Watling!

This...this scene is really creepy. I blame the music. And pretty much everything else.

Seriously, this doesn't feel like a Doctor Who story. It feels like a gothic horror story. And maybe that's the point...

Suddenly, BALLS. Balls that...change the Yeti prop completely, apparently.

99

Sandwiches. Sandwiches. Sandwiches.

Aww, Victoria's not happy about them paying attention to her new dress. Also, SANDWICHES.

"Well, then we ARE landing, aren't we?"
"Let's hope it's somewhere pleasant!"
"Hey, it might even be Scotland!"
#jamieee

And then the TARDIS magically started forming cobwebs. In Space.

Ah, so THIS must be the titular Web. I was wondering what webs had to do with Yeti in the Underground.

Wait a minute...soldiers...and a dead colonel...OH MY GOD PLEASE TELL ME WE'RE ABOUT TO SEE...

Jamie. I don't quite understand how your socks and boots work. Also, your boots = SHINY.

So I guess Two said the magic words: the web's gone now.

"Shall we go out and have a look?"
"Now is it safe?"
"Oh, I shouldn't think so for a moment."
Typical Doctor. Typical typical Doctor.

Looks like an abandoned Underground station to me. #RAVALOX

NO JAMIE NO NO NO DON'T TOUCH THE RAILS whew okay the electricity's off. Somehow the possible life-or-death situation just now makes the humor of Jamie not knowing what electricity is a lot less effective.

Wait. Soldiers with power cables...are they going to blow something up?

Yup. Boxes o' s'plosives. And YETI!

Oh god. Seriously. That woman. Has the creepiest evil grin.

So apparently the Yeti have...guns now...that shoot webs...what.

No s'plosion, but now the boxes are glowing a lot. That must be some REALLY strong web.

You know, considering how Jamie thinks that Two might be, you know, *dead* and everything, I'm surprised he isn't flipping out more.

Gunshots and Yeti? This can only mean one thing: YETI.

Agh, echo-y voices make for hard of hearing things D:

Ah, so THAT'S what the inside of a Yeti sphere looks like! And Now We Know.

Travers and TARDIS crew reunite! Actually, I think Travers might be the first non-villain returning character in Classic Who.

Well, Victoria seems to recognize him. And now, of course, the obligatory "...it can't be..."

Aw, and Jamie is a happy puppy now :3

"And you met him in 1935, in Tibet?" And this story takes place nearly 40 years later? OH HI UNIT DATING CONTROVERSY FANCY MEETING YOU HERE

Aw, poor Plucky Inquisitive Journalist Guy. He just wants his story but the mean military and science people won't let him have it.

"In short, you are a sensationalist!" Maybe I take that back.

FOOTAGE! Hello, giant monster killer Yeti! Whoosa big fluffy cuddly behemoth of death? Yesshu are! Yesshu are!

It'd be more efficient to count stories where Team TARDIS DOESN'T get blamed for everything for being in the wrong place at the wrong time.

Soldier, I think you may be onto something with the whole "the Yeti come from space" thing. Because, you know, they kinda do.

Ah, the London Underground. I wonder how much (if at all) that map has changed since this story was made. *has weird fantasy about "what if this story took place in the New York subways"*

Oh my god. I want New Who to do a Yeti-in-the-Subway story now. It would be like Daleks in Manhattan, except not.

Uh oh, Victoria's gone out into the tunnels on her own. Somehow I don't see this going down well.

Sounds like someone singing scales...GEE, I WONDER IF THAT COULD BE A RECORDER-LESS TWO.

Oh. Actually, it isn't at all.

Well, looks like Jamie can read now. (I don't remember if canon said he could or not but I know about a Short Trip where he couldn't write.)

I just realized: I don't think Pat was in this episode at all. Wonder if he was on vacation again.

Also, as the Master would say, WEEEEEEEEEEEB!

Well, they've nailed the pyramid-thing from the last story, now what? WEEEEEEEEB.

"Doctor, is that you?" It is! And OH MY GOD IT'S FINALLY HIM....

Ladies and Gentlemen: the man, the legend, the mustache, Alistair Gordon Lethbridge-Stewart. Or, as we all know him, The Brig.

Okay, so technically he isn't a Brigadier yet, but BRIG. #BRIG

"Where did the colonel come from?"
"...I don't know."
Well, when a mommy colonel and a daddy colonel love each other very much...

You know, I'm really glad that hat didn't stick around. Not too keen on it.

Jamie and Evans must pause for a moment in their journey because CHOCOLATE.

"Look, all you want to do is save your own skin!"
"Well, it's the only one I got!"

Slide show! "Those Yeti have changed in appearance!" Huh, maybe the redesign is going to be part of the plot.

Doctor Who's had a lot of base-under-siege stories, but this probably resonated especially well because of the familiar location.

Well, okay, familiar to Londoners. Can't remember many Tube station names and in NYC the "Circle Line" is a tour boat service, not a train.

This reporter seems to be getting more and more weasel-y, so thank you Brig for so swiftly shanghie-ing him into being your bitch.

("It seems, however, that there's a traitor at large inside the fortress.") DUN DUN DUUUUUUUN.

Yeti in the base! And it's heading for the s'plosives...

Uh oh. Victoria, whatever you just told Chorley, I have a funny feeling you shouldn't have.

Yup, I was right. But JAMIE!

Wait a sec, FOOTAGE! But this can't be a surviving episode, I thought only episode 1 still existed...

But between the Team and the TARDIS, WEEEEEEEEEEEB!

Sorry Two, but WEEEEEEB does not approve of your attempts to Do Science To It!

Ah, of course, this must be surviving censor footage. I can just taste the delicious irony in the air.

And now we've got a traitor mystery story on our hands in addition to the Base Under Siege plot.

"I have a craft...that travels in time and space." Just think, Brig, not too long from now, you'll be the one explaining this to people. "Now this...craft of yours, this time-space craft, could it get us out of here?" Also, I LOVE how readily he accepts the TARDIS's existence.

"Well I've heard some stories in my time but that one really."
"So you don't believe him?"
"No of course not, sir! The whole idea is screwy! A police box?"
"Well whether you think it foolish or not, we are going to rescue that craft."
"Oh, but sir!"
"Captain Knight, the army has failed to defeat this menace, now the Doctor thinks he might succeed. Personally, I doubt it, but if we stay here we're as good as dead. Therefore, I do not intend to leave any escape route unexplored, no matter how...'screwy' you may think it."

Another difficulty in slogging through recons is you usually have a much foggier idea of the layout of wherever they are.

I still don't completely understand where this suspicion towards Evans is coming from. He seems more of the I-just-want-out kind of weasel.

Wait. Wait. Wait wait wait wait. If the whole point of rescuing the TARDIS was so they could escape, then how did they get to the surface?

Suddenly, YETI! ...But isn't that the Cybermen's music they're playing?

ahkflhaklfhadsklfhdskl this would've made a GREAT surviving episode. Any episode with action scenes like this should've lived.

Okay, well, technically speaking, ALL Doctor Who episodes should've lived, but if I could only save a few...

("The battle seems futile as the colonel orders a retreat.") "Seems?" Which seems to imply that it isn't actually futile?

In the event of Yeti, just rob an electronics store. Because saving the world is Just One Of Those Good Excuses.

Aw, poor Knight. The Yeti tear him down but leave Two alone.

Uh oh, I bet I know where that third Yeti model got to...
("One by one, every last soldier is caught and killed.") All except...
THE BRIG.

I should probably mention that despite Nicholas Courtney's passing,
I refuse to believe the Brig is dead until canon says so.

I mean, Barbara and Ben are still cited as being alive in the present
day even though Jacqueline Hill and Michael Craze died years ago.

Yup, the Brig had the third Yeti model. And then REAL YETI. And
TRAVERS.

Also, this isn't in the recons but you can still hear it, you notice how
the end credits were meant to have the web in them as well?

It was in the surviving episode, though.

"I...am...the Intelligence." The way he started that, I could've sworn
he was going to say "I...am...the Master" a la Derek Jacobi.

I wonder if this sequel story had been planned all along. We never
really learned much about the Intelligence the first time, did we?

Oh...so it just wants the Doctor's smartness? ...Well okay then.

"Well, if what the Intelligence says is true, my mind will be like that
of a child. You've have to look after me...until I grow up."

Excuse me while I am grinning at the image of Jamie and Victoria
parenting baby!Two.

Excuse me while I am grinning even more at Jamie pitching a battle
strategy to the Brig.

Meanwhile, Two and Anne Do Science To It.

"Certainly no sound out there." Except for that random low
humming.

The solution to everything: pounding your fist down on it.

Aww, Two's so happy with his shiny new toy.

This is fun and interesting: father and daughter sharing the screen alone. Oh yeah, and Yeti.

So I wonder if Evans is going to turn out to be The Spineless Coward Who Winds Up Saving The Day.

Maybe it's just because I can't see her creeper face anymore, but I'm becoming gradually less suspicious of Anne being the mole.

Oh, this is going to be good: fighting Yeti with Yeti.

So apparently the fungus can break through SOLID WALLS now.

I take back my earlier comment. Maybe Evans is just That Spineless Coward Who Lives A Coward And Dies A Coward.

Kinda like Adelaide in Horror of Fang Rock, but I actually felt bad for her because of how legit scared she was.

I just realized an image I REALLY wish I could see in this serial: Two-running over Underground tracks.

Seriously, that man turns running into a comedic art like no other Doctor (except maybe Matt Smith).

PLEASE TELL ME YETI VS. YETI IS ABOUT TO HAPPEN.

Wait. Did the Brig just knock Two to the ground? As part of a diversion? ...Oh wait, he's still doing that by Battlefield.

"Oh, don't blame yourself, professor."
"Well, why not? I...I've sacrificed you all! And for what?"
Cut to Two playing his recorder.

You know, this literally only just occurred to me: was Pat already an accomplished recorder player, or did he have to learn it for the role?

Huh. This is the first time we've seen Chorley in a good long while.

...and then he takes off his glasses and almost bears a striking resemblance to a late-20-something Matthew Waterhouse. Or is that just me?

Oh. Snap. I think Chorley just cracked the case. And it was the last person I was expecting.

What's this? The Brig being naive? Now this is an odd turn. Of course, he was young and just starting out in the world...

Jamie-in-a-Box! Jamie-in-a-Box!

"Yeti...come towards me..." Oh, come on, Jamie, you can do better than that. Just try calling it like a kitty! Because kitties.

Aww, Jamie is disappoint when Two's toys won't play with him.

So it was Chorley who turned out to be not such a bad guy after all. I applaud you, sir.

OH GOD. YETI WITH JAMIE IN A CHOKEHOLD. NOT SURE HOW OKAY I AM WITH THIS.

"I refuse to submit until you release Jamie!" ...there's a really bad innuendo in there somewhere...

Suddenly, JAMIE AND YETI TO THE RESCUE! Also, wow, Frazer's REALLY getting into the narration here.

Oh wait, that just threw a wrench in Two's plan, I bet...

"YOU BLITHERING WELSH IMBECILE, WHY CAN'T YOU DO WHAT YOU'RE TOLD?" ...did Two just call Jamie Welsh?

Also, WOW. Forget Frazer being really into the narration, Troughton is throwing EVERYTHING into this scene.

Seriously, this is the first time I've heard Two so angry that he sounds almost close to tears.

And now it's time for the extremely hurried goodbye. Those were certainly a lot more common in Two's day than others, wasn't it?

In Loving Memory of Nicholas Courtney

Originally Posted May 19th, 2011

FURY FROM THE DEEP

Written by Victor Pemberton
Aired: March 16 – April 20, 1968

Pat, I love you, but the sooner I finish up these recons the better. So let's do our FINAL completely-missing serial: Fury From the Deep!

Well, yes technically there are still some surviving clips like...the TARDIS falling out of the sky and landing on the surface of the ocean?

"Trust ye to bring us RIGHT down in the middle of the sea!" Jamie, YOUR HAIR. Two, YOUR HAT.

If there's one thing you see a lot in the TCP, it's publicity stills from this serial. Because of Two's hat.

Aaaaand there's Jamie and Victoria calling the Doctor out on always landing on Earth/England. Also, JAMIE'S REVERSIBLE COW-VEST.

Awwww, foam-fight!

"What's this?"
"It's the sonic screwdriver. Never fails."
Except on wood. But I digress. SONIC SCREWDRIVER!

Jeez, what is it with people aiming crosshairs at Two when he's trying to have a nice day at the beach?

And this time it actually hits him!

Awww, puppy-pile. Which would be a lot more adorable if they didn't have guns pointed at them.

Well, I think we know who the Snarky Asshole Commander of this story is going to be...

Ah, hello Mrs. Harris! I don't think we get to see the spouses of important supporting characters in Classic serials very often.

The more these guys talk about stuff getting into the pipelines, the more I think playing around in the foam was a bad idea.

("In the bunk room, Jamie is standing on the Doctor's shoulders.") As per usual. They must have nice views from there. #stupidkiltjokes

Victoria's lockpicking skills > all of Jamie, apparently. Ouch.

Stinging seaweed in your folder? Ouch. That must be like accidentally grabbing a jellyfish. In your underwear drawer.

Huh. I thought Victoria was supposed to be a nervous wreck by this story. She certainly still seems spry, witty, and active.

See? She's even trying to fix the sabotage in the oxygen valve room. Where she's now trapped.

VENTILATION SHAFT, YOU ARE DRUNK.

Victoria is rescued and...Jamie what do you have pressed against your face?

Aaaaand Mrs. Harris' sting mark has mysteriously vanished. How convenient. For the seaweed.

Ugh. That bubbling sound from the seaweed is actually making my stomach feel queasy...

Wow. That's some surprisingly intricate wall design for a pantry. Especially a pantry in Classic Who.

("Cut off from the influence of the weed...") Umm...did you guys stop and think about how that would sound?

Oh wow. Thanks to Turn Left, apparently I can't hear "the south of England" without thinking "flooded with radiation."

Ah, hello Suspicious Looking/Sounding Maintenance Workers! (Oh crap, one of them must be Mr. Quill...)

Dear Mr. Oak, you have the creepiest voice ever. -Hannah

You know what this scenario kinda reminds me of? Inferno. All this talk about pressure build-ups and gas, etc.

shudder Maybe it's the music, but that image of Mr. Oak's arm covered in seaweed freaks me out WAAAAY more than it really should.

OH DEAR GOD NOT THIS SCENE. THIS. SCENE.

Okay, so that wasn't as bad as Miss Evangelista's warped face in Forest of the Dead, but still pretty damn creepy.

Well, looks like we may finally have someone sensible besides Mr. Harris trying to convince the higher ups that something's wrong here.

Ah. FINALLY Two and company find the malicious seaweed. 'Bout time. (Yes I know it's only the second episode, but still.)

"Why should anyone want me to get stung by a piece of seaweed?" #curiousquotes

Okay, maybe NOW Robson will believe that there's something alive down there. Alive and foamy.

So naturally when Victoria mentions "like a spider," my eye is drawn to my old high school graduation tassel swaying in the breeze...

Wow. WOW. Robson, you are a stubborn ass. A REALLY REALLY stubborn ass.

Huh. I think this is one of the few times in Doctor Who that the crew gets back to the TARDIS with stuff to Do Science To It.

(I mean that in the sense that the TARDIS is usually inaccessible for most of the story for one reason or another.)

"A harmless old man and a couple of teenagers?" ...You know, I think that's the first time I've ever heard Team Two referred to like that.

I know Jamie's and Victoria's ages are never specified on screen (correct me if I'm wrong), but I always thought they were young adults. Well...okay, seventeen or eighteen at the youngest.

Huh. Usually takes until about the penultimate episode for the crazy boss to finally lose it, but Robson seems to be jumping on that early.

Okay, so maybe he hasn't "finally lost it" yet, but he's certainly yelling more intensely in this scene than he has so far.

"He's cracking up, Harris." Or maybe I was right the first time.

And the solution is found not just by science, but by mythology. Well, not really the solution, but certainly an answer.

Ohhhhh yes, Robson is definitely losing it. Rapid-fire cured ham.

Seriously, Mr. Oak and Mr. Quill are some of the biggest creeps to ever creep on this show. And that's saying a LOT.

Okay, so I have to ask: if Victoria has such proficient lock-picking skills, why haven't we seen her use them before? Or have I forgotten?

Finally, companion screaming is good for something: fending off the Monster of the Week.

Another one of those action scenes I REALLY wish had survived. I want to see Jamie standing on a kitchen table D:

"Doctor why is it that we always end up in trouble?"
"Victoria, it's the spice of life, my dear!"
"Well I'm not so sure."

Uh oh, first sign.

So now Two's finally gotten to announce to everyone about the monster seaweed. Maybe now they can actually DO something about it.

Despite what just happened, that might be one of the calmest Who cliffhangers I've ever seen.

The music in this scene is sounding particularly 8-bit. Or maybe that's just the main melody line.

Awwwwww, sleeping Jamie.

I really REALLY wish I could see this scene. Jamie's sounding even more empathetic than usual and I just wish I could see his FACE...

"He looks so peaceful out there, doesn't he?" ...you mean Jamie sleeping? Aww.

Poor Victoria. Once in a while we get a companion who truly, deeply just wants to go somewhere *nice* for a change.

Evelyn made this same speech in Arrangements For War and Sarah Jane had a similar one right before she left. Who else...?

Aw crap. Mr. Oak and Mr. Quill are still running free. When is someone going to realize that they're, well, toxic?

Suddenly, FOOTAGE! ...Yikes, what a way to go.

"Jamie, you wouldn't let me go down there on my own, now would you?"
"Well, ye...uh...well...well, noooo...oh..."
#comealongpuppy

Fact: Mr. Oak and Mr. Quill will never not be creepy as hell. Ever.

Jamie's Scotty Senses are tingling. They're saying, "EVIL."

Mr. Oak, please. never. speak. again.

I just realized: Jamie's face and respiratory system may be safe from the gas and the seaweed but his legs certainly aren't.

A mass of bubbling white foam surges up the shaft. (And that was my one dirty joke for the evening.)

Okay. I've officially concluded that Oak and Quill are the kind of villain I hate because they're SO GOOD at being really nasty.

Actually, I feel the exact same way about the Dream Lord. Maybe that's why Amy's Choice made me feel so...uncomfortable.

On the other hand, I'm on the boat of fan theorists who want him to turn out to be a pre-Valeyard.

FINALLY they've got more concrete confirmation of foam-invasion. I think that's the first time I've ever heard "fantastic" used negatively.

Oh hey, look who decided to come back to the party! Hello, Robson! My my, you're not looking or sounding very sane at all, are you?

"I'm afraid that Mr. Robson is being controlled by some force that emanates from this weed." #roesloveddrugs

"Victoria! ...Victoria...say something...no...no, ye can't be dead... Victoria...oh, if anything happened to you I'd never forgive myself."

"...Jamie, I didn't know you cared." #allofmycreys #also #moodwhiplash #emotionallycockblocked

Seaweed invasion? Natural reaction: GROUP CLING!
"It's begun. The battle of the giants!" *DUN DUN DUUUUUN*

Okay, NOW I think we finally know what Oak and Quill's original roles on the rigs were.

"Now supposing that person was under the control of the weed..." I'm not even going to make the joke because you all know what it is.

I love it when bad guys' weaknesses are just an overdose of some mundane thing, like oxygen.

Actually, wasn't oxygen how they drove out the Marshmen in Full Circle?

Nice helmet, dude. Put some red on that and you could try out for the guards on Gallifrey.

Aw, this scene between Ms. Jones and Robson might even be sweet if I could actually see it.

Wait, never mind, she's being strict again.

Wait, never never mind, he's actually responding to her now.

Jamie, don't hush the lady when she has a legitimate concern, especially one like this.

Was that a vent's-eye-view we just got? Don't see those all the time on this show.

More footage! So I have to ask, how did they account for all the deaths in the overseas edit if they censored all the shots of actual death? Did they just...leave the screen black or something? I dunno, I think that's what they did in the German edit of Naruto...

Jamie to the rescue again! This time, taking down the creepers at last!

"Eh, there's a wee bit o' power left in the ol' McCrimmon punch yet." The O'l McCrimmon Punch. #theolmccrimmonpunch

So. I guess this means that Jamie Punch is canon now?

Wow. This story really isn't treating Victoria very well, is it?

Although I honestly don't understand what Robson hopes to achieve by kidnapping her. A hostage for bargaining, maybe?

FOOTAGE!

Yup, she's his hostage. And Robson is somehow slightly less of a Shouty Man now.

Hello, looks like we're about to have an aerial chase!

"Come on in! The water's lovely!" And by "water," you mean "deadly mind-control foam" oh god Two why are you jumping into that.

Come into my parlor, said the Robson to the Doc.

"Matter will never conquer mind! It's against the law of nature!" Really? I thought that was just philosophy.

So after all the clings Two gets, he very nearly gets a Hug of Death.

Ahhhhhh, that's right: Victoria's screaming actually has some legit effect on the monsters in this story.

You know you might conceivably be screwed when your best chance for escape is someone who's never flown a helicopter but REALLY wants to.

Especially when he calls it a "primitive" machine and STILL can't fly it properly.

WOAH. Now I have to wonder if this footage of the helicopter in flight was just stock footage the reconner found.

(To clarify the "WOAH," the copter just flipped upside down for a couple seconds.)

"Well I was under the impression you couldn't loop-de-loop in a helicopter." OR MAYBE THAT WAS SURVIVING FOOTAGE WHAT.

Ah, yes, thank you: some much-needed backseat piloting from the other guy.

Okay, I know I've said this a bajillion times already, but I REALLY WISH I COULD *SEE* THIS SCENE.

"Just one thing: I've got it up alright...and it should be encouragingly simple to propel it forward...erm...however...how do I land it?"

And the solution to defeating this foamy, weedy menace? NOOOIIIIIIIIIISE.

And not just any noise, but Victoria's screaming. For once, not a nuisance, but a WEAPON. #awwwyeah

Oh FFS Victoria, WHAT'S THIS ABOUT NOT BEING ABLE TO SCREAM WHEN WE ACTUALLY NEED IT? ...oh. Thank you, that's better.

More surviving footage of the foam! But wait, why would THAT clip need to be censored? No one died or got attacked or anything...

Ahhhh, so THIS is what those gajillion pictures of Team Two making weird faces come from!

Oh wow, lots of surviving footage from this scene! :D

Screaming as a weapon...I'm kinda glad I'm watching this episode in broad daylight.

Hey, it's Mrs. Harris! And Robson is...completely sane again? Okay, I'll admit I wasn't expecting that...

Awww, happy celebration dinner! Also, dayum, the Harris' have a FINE house.

"And to think, I wanted to keep you locked up, Doctor!"
"Well, lots of people have tried."

Here it comes, the decision to leave...any minute now...

Oh wow. This is going very cordially and Two seems to be taking it pretty well. Jamie, I'm not so sure about.

"Now, Jamie, she must make up her own mind, it's her own life, it's her decision."

On another note, I'm ASTOUNDED that Robson was allowed to return to his post after all this. I mean, seriously.

"Jamie...you wouldn't go...without saying goodbye, would you?"
"Of course not. That won't be till the morning, anyway. ...Goodnight, Victoria."
"Goodnight, Jamie."

#ohgod #mycreys

Okay. I swear to god I heard a kiss in there. There's nothing in the narration about it, but I HEARD SOMETHING THAT SOUNDED LIKE A KISS.

("Victoria watches as her friends disappear out of sight and out of her life. Back in the TARDIS, Jamie looks sadly at Victoria's image...")

"Oh, come on, let's go."
"Well, where would you like to go?"
"I couldn't care less."
"I was fond of her too, you know."

Goddammit. That didn't make me cry, but it sure made me feel things. #feeeeelings

Well, goodbye, Victoria. You will be missed. Actually, you get to meet up with the Brig and Sarah Jane in Downtime, don't you?

Originally Posted June 3rd, 2011

CHARACTER RETROSPECTIVE: VICTORIA

Victoria Sweet-Cybermat-Shooting-Flower Waterfield. Of all the companion introductions on the show, I still find hers to be the most unintentionally hilarious. She wasn't introduced as just a damsel-in-distress, she was a princess locked in a tower by monsters and had to be rescued by a dashing young warrior and whisked away on his (blue wooden time-traveling) steed. Like Susan, I have mixed feelings about Victoria as a companion. On one hand, I feel like she's inadequately equipped for adventuring in time and space. On the other hand, I think most of her appeal comes from her social aspects and her actions as, well, a person. Victoria is very much a young woman of her time. She's best at being social, getting to know people, and using the power of words. Like Polly before her, she always tries to appeal to the humanity in the story's opponents. Victoria is much more of a lover than a fighter. Unless you're a Cybermat, in which case, as one of my TPC friends aptly put it: "she will shoot you in the tum."

In retrospect, Victoria was probably one of the best examples in Classic Who of a realistic and almost deconstructive look at what it means to be a companion in her situation. She's by no means the only companion to come aboard the TARDIS because she has nowhere else to go, but she's one of the few who is eventually worn down by the experience instead of strengthened by it. And from a storytelling aspect, that doesn't have to be a bad thing. Actually, I wouldn't mind an approach like that for a companion in New Who where they take a more modern and critical approach to companions who leave because they Just Can't Take It Anymore (and before anyone cites Martha Jones as an example of this, I think she chose to leave *because* of how much she was bettered by her time with the Doctor, and recognized when it would be healthy to remove herself and apply her skills beyond the TARDIS). Watching Victoria leave was sad, both because of how dear she obviously was to both Two and Jamie, but also because of the harsh truth that her leaving was the best thing for her. Sometimes I wonder if the survival of more footage from Victoria's era would have helped in establishing a more concrete conclusion about certain aspects of her character, particularly her relationship with Jamie. While there's still evidence in the dialogue and certain actions that Victoria and Jamie had a certain affection for each other, I still wish I could actually *see* more of it. There's a lot you can glean from just watching the physical acting.

As I neared the end of Victoria's run, Elisabeth Sladen passed away. As the whole fandom was in mourning for the tragic and unexpected loss of our beloved Sarah Jane Smith, I had to take a short break from my commentaries because being on Twitter and Tumblr was just too depressing. Still, I wanted to do something happy and Who-related to help cheer myself up, so I decided to watch a couple episodes from the Lost in Time box set with the audio commentaries on. One of them was the surviving episode of The Abominable Snowmen, where Deborah Watling talked with Gary Russell about her time as Victoria. It was just the antidote I needed. Deborah went gleefully on about her friendship with Frazer Hines, the loving family atmosphere on set and, of course, Yeti cuddles. She was also at Regenerations 2011, where her agent marveled at the little cartoon I'd made of Two's Girls and asked if I did art professionally. While Deborah was signing it, I got to thank her for indirectly helping me through Lis Sladen's loss. She was also delightfully surprised that I was such a big fan of the Yeti.

THE WHEEL IN SPACE

Written by David Whitaker and Kit Pedler
Aired: April 17 – June 1, 1968

Okay, only two more recons left. Let's do this: THE WHEEL IN SPACE!

Technically I watched this over a year ago, but it was just the two surviving episodes (they were on Netflix Instant for some reason).

Now, time to do this properly. Or at least as close to "properly" as you can get with orphaned Who.

Oh no, don't put us through Victoria's departure again. I'm reading Push right now, I don't need another sad D:

Wait...the TARDIS scanner is showing them "temptations?" I thought this was Doctor Who, not ancient mythology.

Oh, those wacky fluid links, always causing a ruckus.

I'm assuming that that mercury gas is the TARDIS's way of saying "GTFO, I need to do repairs."

Hey. Hey Jamie. Nice ascot. And cow vest.

After watching 2001: A Who Odyssey, I can't picture that robot as anything other than a squat, walking version of HAL 9000.

(BTW, if you've never seen A Who Odyssey, do right now. It's AMAZING.)

And Jamie tells Two to "stick his rod back in and" no. I'm stopping this joke right here.

This scenario of landing on a supposed ghost ship floating in space is starting to remind me of Girl in the Fireplace a bit.

"Well, right now I'd like a nice plate of roast beef with all the trimmings." AHFKAHDFKLSHFKLDHSKLFDSHFKLDS #in-jokes

Ah yes, this is Jamie's first exposure to space food, isn't it? So, was he just not eating from the food dispenser on the TARDIS? #confuse

Unless the Doctor replaced the TARDIS food machine with an actual kitchen or something...

Two, you might have to clarify what you mean by the late 20th century having "very few wars."

Okay, so I know they never really specified the date in Fury, but I was always under the assumption that that's when it took place.

Is Two using his recorder as a telescope? But more importantly, awwwwwwww, sleeping!Jamie.

("The Doctor covers him with a metallic blanket.") #AAAWWWWW

Yup, this thing is HAL.

fjkalfjhlkashfdkls I keep expecting that static to clear and show a Weeping Angel. Dammit, Moff.

JAMIE MCCRIMMON YOU ARE WEARING A COW.

Ooooo, fly away, pretty balls!

HAL 9000: 0. Jamie McCrimmon: 1.

Oh yay, they actually do us the courtesy of introducing the local characters by name this time!

Agh, I'd forgotten we weren't actually on the Wheel yet.

desperately tries to avoid making a comment about eggs and sperm

X-rays always sound cool until they're about to blow up the main characters.

Oh wow. Tanya's accent is so wonderfully Russian, but the things she's saying with it...aren't.

So I wonder if Two has taught Jamie Morse code or if he's just going "A SHINY THING WILL SAVE US!"

OH WAIT NEVER MIND IT'S MAKING THINGS WORSE OH GOD JAMIE PLEASE DON'T EXPLODE THEIR HEADS.

Ah, they're figuring it out now. Whew. (Okay, so maybe it's not Morse code, but it's some sort of pattern.)

Safe! Except for the Mystery of the Floating Space Eggs.

Is it just me, or is the wall patterned with pictures of corn cobs? #hannahnoticesweirdthings

"Well, I'll tell you what, eh? If you get scared I'll...I'll let you hold my hand, okay?"
"I'm serious."
"So am I."

"Violating the outer skin" of the Wheel? Please stop making the sexual analogies even easier to make than they already are.

Speaking of outer skin, HELLO JAMIE'S CHEST.

I've probably missed it if it's happened before, but is this the first time we hear Jamie's full name?

"And your friend?"
"Uhh...the Doctor."
"I can't put that down."
"Uhh...John Smith."

Jamie, I don't think you know the legacy you've started.

Ahhhhh, that answers my question from nearly a year ago about where the name John Smith came from.

I'd wondered if Susan had got it from that band she was listening to in An Unearthly Child, but it was Jamie looking at a medical box label.

MYSTERY SOLVED. #mythBUSTED

"I'll tell Zoe to show you around." Zoe? ZOE!!!
Aww, Zoe's such a little technobabbler, isn't she?

I'm sorry, I can't hear you over the sound of this being my new favorite companion-companion introductory conversation.

"Your clothes! You're wearing female garments!"
"Female? Look, I'll have you know this is a kilt. Have you not seen it before?"
"Kilt? Kilt...a barbaric form of garment as worn by a kiltie! Are you of Scandinavian origin? Danish?"
"No I'm not! I'm a true-bred Scot..."
"Oh, Scot! Scotland, of course. Pre-century history isn't my field, you see."
"Aye, well maybe not but just you watch your lip or I'll put you across my knee and larrup you."
"Oh this IS going to be fun. I shall learn a lot from you! Come on James Robert McCrimmon!"

I can just hear the cogs in Jamie's head working: "och, too much science..."

Looks like Jarvis is going to be the Stubborn Paranoid One of this story...

Tanya, the things you say are weird and they confuse me. We get it, your nose is special.

Awww, hatching babby Cybermans! *pictures little Cyberchild asking its mother where Cyberbabies come from*

And so concludes THIRTEEN STRAIGHT EPISODES OF RECON OH GOD.

that awkward moment when I remember that I HAVE actually seen this episode before, it's just been over a year

Umm, Jamie I still don't understand what you were sabotaging the ray gun for.

Meanwhile in Cybermenland, I think this is the first time we've seen them with the teardrop formation on their eyes.

Also, when do they drop those voices? Seriously, I don't know what it is, but something about these voices really bugs me.

N'awwww, cybermat! Wook at dat cute widdle worm of death...

Two, you're awake! Pat, you're back from vacation!

I feel like a dumbass now. Of *course* Jamie didn't want them to blow up the rocket because THE TARDIS WAS STILL ONBOARD.

This is a Two's Trix Cereal Suspenders Appreciation Post.

I think I've said this before, but I have to praise Classic Who for usually getting an international crew for their space station stories.

Awww, big meanie's picking on Zoe for her braininess.

Okay dude, I'm beginning to think that keeping your new pet a secret is a very bad idea.

Especially now that THEY'RE BREEDING.

Seeing a real episode for the first time in a while is rapidly rekindling my appreciation for Patrick Troughton's face.

I can just feel Jamie's fed-up-ness with science radiating off the screen.

"Logic, my dear Zoe, merely enables one to be wrong with authority." #moreclassiclines

Oh right, I forgot: only the Cyberleader-brain-head-thing has the voice that really bugs me for some reason in this story.

I have this weird appreciation for the fact that you can VERY clearly tell that the cybermats' feelers are just jagged sheets of styrofoam.

Ah, I remember this scene! So much overacting from one guy...

"It sounded as if all the devils in Hell were hounding someone..." Huh. Didn't know they could say "Hell" on kid's television back then.

I can also feel Jamie's burning need to out-brain Zoe radiating off the screen.

Aww, so much appreciation for that string of subtle glances between the crew members. (I'm saying "appreciation" a lot this time, aren't I?)

Somehow I get the feeling that those two guys going off to inspect the rocket aren't going to come back alive.

Oh riiiiiight, I forgot this is where the Cybermen have those head-mounted control beam things.

"...but now they're more robot than man." #darthvader

Okay, I can understand a story's need for a disagreeable jerky boss character, but do they always need to be this extreme?

Or maybe I'm just thinking that because Jarvis is basically Robson from the last serial in space.

Well, the cyber-possession might not be evident in the victim's movements, but surely their voices must be giving something away?

Jamie has had enough of this Science. So he's gonna be all up in your face like "WHATCHA DOIN? WHATCHA DOIN? WHATCHA DOIN?"

Ah yes, the good ol' cassette-tapes-in-the-future trope.

You know, I think Two was more frightened than flattered at hearing Gemma calling his head "extraordinary."

"Are there any ordinary circumstances in space?" Why isn't this one of Two's more classic lines? Oh right... #burninatedepisodes

"Someone just used the incinerator in the loading bay." ...Oh. I think we know what happened to that body now.

Okay, so maybe they *are* starting to notice that something's up with their voices.

I forget, have they established yet how long Zoe's been on the Wheel? Or is she just not good at reading people at the start?

"Do you ever feel anything emotional, Zoe?"
"Emotional?"
Well, that answers that question.

"My head's been pumped full of facts and figures which I reel out automatically when needed but...well, I want to FEEL things as well!"

I just realized: Bechdel Test, PASSED.

Ah, good ol' Two catching on to the whole cyber-possession thing before he'd even met the victims.

I'm not sure why I'm only noticing this now, but we're starting to build up quite a body count here, aren't we?

"What's the thing that we need to survive which the Cybermen don't?"
"Food!"
"Always thinking of your stomach, aren't you?"

("The Doctor and Jamie stand close together.") Scary little metal beasties? CLING!

Awww, little cybermats go boom!

Well, unlike Robson, Jarvis didn't explode into mental breakage. He just sort of...stopped.

Ah, so this must be where Jamie inadvertently convinces Zoe to leave the Wheel and go off adventuring with them...

More censored footage! Yeah, a guy putting his hands on another guy's neck like that, I can understand.

...and rather silently banging his head against a door...

Just noticing that one of the guys here has REALLY shiny hair.

OH WAIT. I REMEMBER THAT FOOTAGE OF THE METEORS NOW.

Come to think of it, I might've done commentaries for the two surviving episodes already but didn't save them because it was incomplete.

Because I'm pretty sure I remember remarking about all the action I missed in episodes 4 and 5...

That alarm sounds really familiar. It sounds almost exactly the same as the Yeti's web guns in "The Web of Fear," amongst other things.

("The meteorites come rushing through space, tumbling one after the other in all different shapes and sizes.") All shapes being spherical.

So all this buildup about the Cybermen's plans was just coming to "they want to plunder Earth for its minerals?" ...well okay then.

I keep forgetting how worried!Jamie is one of the adorablest things ever.

Jamie and Zoe out for a nice little potentially deadly spacewalk. Fun times!

"This controls the oxygen of the space station." ...Lava lamps? Well, it was the 60's, I guess.

Oh, it's just background stuff. Never mind.

FOOTAGE. AND THOSE ARE DEFINITELY LAVA LAMPS.

WHAT. GEMMA NOOOO! DDDD:

In other news...

HAHAHAHAHA YES I'M FINALLY DONE WITH RECONS UNTIL THE SPACE PIRATES! ...oh wait, I've already watched most of the interim stuff already...

Awww, Jamie and Zoe's little space dance.

I just realized: it feels rather out of character for the Doctor to be deliberately throwing his companions into danger like this.

Of course, I'm saying this coming off of Matt Smith getting through a whole army to rescue one of his companions...

Oh right, Two's calling "needs of the many over the needs of the few" on this one.

And now back to your regularly scheduled programming of Cybermen Killing People.

When Tanya was saying "turn it off," it almost sounded like "damn it all." Of course, that would've worked too.

ZOE. THAT SPACE SUIT LOOKS GIANT ON YOU. YOU ARE SMALL. YOU ARE NOT A BIG PERSON.

Wow. They somehow got away with a boom mike being very visible at the top of the screen. Didn't notice until they pulled it out of the shot.

I just realized: these Cybermen have had their Wiffle ball joints replaced with something actually resembling technology. #SCIENCE

Probably missed it, but why is the Cyberleader saying "negative" after everyone's name?

Also, it is just me, or does that dark-haired guy next to Leo look like a merger of Two and Adric's brother Varsh? #hannahnoticesweirdthings

Ah. Finally had a good look at the "corncobs" on the walls. Not a weird design, just the shadows.

That might just be the biggest ventilation shaft the Doctor's ever had the pleasure of crawling through. This is also reminding me that Patrick Troughton was rather a small man, but quite charmingly so.

Oh hey, all the writing's in K-9 font! #imsureithasanactualname #butidontknowwhatitis

Again, is it just me, or do these Cybermen always show that they're talking by rocking back and forth slightly?

"I...I think I've got...company."
"...Company? W-what did he mean...COMPANY?!?"
This is a Jamie McCrimmon Appreciation Post.

Pat. Pat. Your face. You look like a defeated puppy. I can't. How do you exist. Your powers are too great.

Also, Jamie's shifty-eyes. #somanywonderfulfaces

Dancing Cybermen. In Space. What. No, I'm serious. They are dancing in space.

Awww, and the happy couple gets to stay together.

And we have our first little genius stowaway! OH SO THIS IS WHERE THAT IMAGE OF TWO AS SAILOR GALLIFREY COMES FROM.

Originally Posted June 14th, 2011

THE DOMINATORS

Written by Mervyn Haisman and Henry Lincoln (as Norman Ashby)
Aired: August 10 – September 1968

How to Start a Story: Characters appear, explain their intentions in detail, and state their names to each other for our convenience.

Ahhhh, so these are the Men Wearing Curtains that my Tumblr friends were talking about.

In other news, welcome to the Island of Death! It's full of poison and deadliness and deathy death death!

I'm still trying to figure out the best way to describe the outfits here. It's like if heavy-curtain weavers were trying to make togas.

Yikes. The Quarks may be cute, but the graphics of their death rays is pretty damn creepy.

FINALLY the TARDIS. And I thought Two talking about "projecting mental images" was actually "giving those men lemons." I don't even know.

Awww, I love how this Team TARDIS is so much more beach-prone than all the others. Countdown till things go wrong...

131

You never know when you'll need a lawn chair and a beach ball while traveling through time and space.

Wow. For black-and-white Who, that was a pretty impressive explosion.

"Looks like some sort of museum."
"Yes, you're right again, Zoe: a WAR museum!"
DRAMATIC PULL-BACK TO REVEAL...a couple guns on a table.

Ah yes, all this talk of atomic warfare: the 60's indeed.

"They've outlawed war!" Outlawed war? OUTLAWED war? Outlawed WAR? HOW DO YOU EVEN OUTLAW WAR?

Considering the Quarks were supposed to be the new Daleks, I can see some story parallels already. Notably all the radiation stuff.

Not sure why the student girl needs to be reciting the planet's history word-for-word. Can't she just tell us the SparkNotes version?

Also, is it really necessary for Rago and Toba to keep saying their names to each other? They're the only ones there.

Still trying to figure out if their outfit is supposed to make them look like a specific shape. They're kind of...domed.

"Yer not thinking what I think you're thinking, are you?"
"That, I think, Jamie, depends on what you think I AM thinking."

AAAAWWWWW THE QUARKS HAVE THE CUTEST VOICES. C'MERE YOU LITTLE SPIKY BOXES OF DEATH.

Wow. Rago and Toba have the most psychedelic monitor screens ever.

Ouch. The clinger has become the clung. That wall's very attracted to you, Jamie.

A bit daft to automatically assume that Two and Jamie are the same species, isn't it?

I'm becoming increasingly convinced that Dulcian art and fashion was modeled after the Greeks and Romans. #TOGAS

I know this story gets panned a lot, but I'm actually really liking the character set-up they have for Cully.

Well, the Quarks may have cuter voices, but they're harder to understand than the Daleks.

PLAY WITH THESE BLOCKS OR WE'LL SHOCK YOU. PLAAAAY.

"Just act stupid. Do you think you can manage that?"
"Oh aye, it's easy."

Science: You're Doing It Wrong.

"How many of these Clever Ones are there?"
"Well, there're not many, you see, we don't like them much. They tell us what to do, you see."

And yet all I can think about is how Pat's hair appears to be ballooning into a big fluffy mushroom.

Ah. The Quarks have now officially been incorporated into Jamie's Registry of Nasty Beasties.

After all that, the Dominators let Two and Jamie leave of their own accord, more or less. ...Well okay then.

I love how Zoe calls out the dresses for being "impractical." Also, she and Cully seem to like holding hands a lot.

On the other hand, Zoe, trust me, you're being a LOT more practical than most other Classic female companions by not wearing HEELS.

So I only just realized: FINALLY we have men (other than Jamie) wearing skirts above the knee!

Well, okay, I've noticed since the beginning that all Dulcians wear dresses/skirts, but some of them are about as long as Jamie's kilt.

Dulcians have two hearts! #TIMELORDS

Apparently the Quarks need to stop every once in a while to "recharge." Good. Give our heroes a chance to escape getting asploded.

So this must be that scene they were talking about on TARDIS Tavern where Zoe's outfit becomes "a little too see-through."

Actually, I'm going to take this moment to regress to an elementary school student so I can make the following joke:

I see Dulkis, I see France, I see Zoe's underpants.

Another weird thing I've noticed about Rago and Toba, they almost never look at each other while talking.

"Why should these people wish us harm?" Because, my dear sir, they are dicks.

With this plan of stealing ancient guns, I'm suddenly getting flashbacks to The Space Museum.

According to Wikipedia, the Dulcians' laid-back and peaceful manner was based on hippie subculture. Huh...

Wait. Two. You LITERALLY just saw a Quark at the survey station. WHY did you need Jamie to remind you of this fact?

Also hey are those Jelly Babies. That bag looks like Jelly Babies.

I swear, Zoe's being the spitting image of Vicki in this scene.

Well, maybe not the SPITTING image since I think the people from The Space Museum were preparing a revolt already, but you know what I mean.

Meanwhile, back to Tech Talk With Two and Jamie.

AND NOW AFTER ALL THESE MONTHS I FINALLY HAVE CONTEXT FOR THAT GIF.

You know, the folks working at the debris site are moving lots of big bricks and rocks, why don't they try attacking the Quarks with those?

The boys have landed. In a manner of speaking. Wow, Pat, those are some flexible legs you've got on you.

"Look at Kando." Well, we would if you'd just change the camera angle so we could see her.

JAMIE I KNOW YOU HAVE GOOD INTENTIONS BUT JUST LET CULLY FIRE THE GUN OH GOD.

Ooooo, Jamie's gonna be a big man now and shoot a gun at the bad man and his beasties.

Wow. That worked pretty well. SHOOT THEM SOME MORE.

Or not.

Wow. See what I meant about eye contact earlier? Rago's standing RIGHT in front of Toba but his eyes are fixed on the ceiling.

Actually, maybe it wasn't the ceiling. Toba's just a few inches taller than Rago.

"I submit." Holy crap. Holy crap holy crap. I actually get to say this:

The Dom has become the Sub.

Oh, hello Jamie and Cully! Hello, conveniently-placed bunker that saved your lives!

You know, considering all the hard manual labor she's had to do so far, I'd say Zoe's having one of the worse First Trips in the TARDIS.

Jamie, I'm not quite sure comparing Quarks to redcoats is really the best analogy.

On the other hand, Bunging A Rock At It seems to be doing something to them after all.

SO THAT'S WHERE THAT ACTION-JAMIE GIF CAME FROM (where we totally don't try to look up Jamie's kilt in slow motion).

Awww, poor Quark. Also, Cully must've had OBSCENELY good aim with that giant boulder at the top of that hill. #seriously

"Somebody destroyed a Quark? But who?"
"Only one person headstrong enough to do that."
"Jamie!"
":DDDD"

So of COURSE Two just HAPPENS to have a Geiger counter to pull out of his pocket and lower into a vent.

You know, I think one of the problems with this story is that the Dominators aren't appealing villains. They're basically just assholes.

Seriously, if that Quark wasn't there I'd be waiting for someone to just punch them in the face.

Out of context, I just have to say: Two be pimpin'.

Meanwhile, back on That Set I Could've Sworn Was From The War Games, the valiant Men in Skirts continue their campaign.

Jamie. What are you even eating. That looks like something I used to buff my nails with.

Also, what are you planning to do with those sheets? Attack disguised as ghosts?

Wait, Two, don't get distracted by the adorable Highlander, keep telling us what the Dominators' plans are!

Okay, covering the Quark's head with a sheet, I guess that works too. OOOOHHHHHH, I think I just figured out what their Evil Plan was all along.

"The whole planet will become one vast molten seething mass of radioactive material!"
"Well, we'll...just have to stop 'em, then."

Well, I have to admit, I never would've seen that one coming.

":DDD Jamie, it's a BRILLIANT idea! It's so simple only you could've thought of it!"
"Oh! ...ayyyye?"
#thesetwo

For a second I thought Two was going to pull a Nine and be all "um, Jamie, I'm trying to resonate concrete," but WAIT HOW IS HE BURNING IT.

Two's doing a lot of Science To It in this scene, isn't he?

So THAT'S where that happy!Two gif comes from! (I've been saying that a lot this serial, haven't I?)

I'm starting to feel bad for the people who had to walk around in the Quark suits. That had to've been rough.

Ho boy, have we actually reached the "just go on and leave me" part of the plot? Don't leave Cully, he's done so much!

Whew, alright, he's safe.

This is actually building to quite a close climax...

Getting the seed off the planet without harming any of "US" at all... Two, are you planning what I think you're planning?

You are. That's...actually quite a dark course of action. Not much of a choice, but still...

"There's just going to be a localized volcanic eruption. It only affects the island."
"Maybe so, but WE happen to be ON the island!"

And so I leave you with one of Patrick Troughton's greatest reaction faces ever.

Originally Posted June 25ᵗʰ, 2011

THE MIND ROBBER

Written by Peter Ling and Derrick Sherwin
Aired: September 14 – October 12, 1968

I'm loving this already. Defiant!Two sits in chair DEFIANTLY!

WOAH WOAH WAIT THE TARDIS JUST BLEW UP WHAT

Verdict: Zoe screams WAY too much.

"Now where in time and space am I?" Guys, I really like Patrick Troughton.

Two's reaction to having both of his companions yelling for help in opposite directions: "No no NO! Not both together! One at a time!"

Wait, why isn't the TARDIS translating for him? Oh wait...it exploded.

Okay wait why is the Doctor suddenly surrounded by creepy children what is this I don't even

Holy crap. I think I've finally found a Doctor Who scene even weirder than the sword-fight in The Christmas Invasion.

The cliffhanger of the episode: the TARDIS crew's about to be IMPALED BY A CHARGING UNICORN. I'm kind of in love with this arc.

They need to do some sort of remake of The Mind Robber for the new series. I'm serious.

"Suddenly, the Doctor picked up a sword and..." HOLY BALLS WHY IS THIS ARC THE BEST THING EVER

They're referencing the year 2000, back when that year was actually far in the future. The best reason why old sci-fi is awesome.

sigh Only one more episode...

"They're no longer human beings! They're fictional characters!" LISTEN. THIS ARC IS FUCKING BRILLIANT.

Don't try and match wits with the Doctor. Ever. ESPECIALLY when he's hooked up to a machine that turns thoughts into reality.

The Doctor and the Master of Fiction are basically having a Pokemon battle with book characters. I couldn't make this up if I tried.

And the final shot is the TARDIS putting itself back together again... why am I so disappointed by that?

Originally Posted February 3rd, 2010

THE INVASION

Written by Derrick Sherwin and Kit Pedler
Aired: November 2 – December 21, 1968

Nearly a year and a half after I first watched The Mind Robber and was disappointed by its last shot I finally get to see what happens next.

ANIMOOTED TEAM TWO!

So they're being attacked by a strange missile from the dark side of the moon? I'll let you guys make your own Transformers jokes.

Suddenly, COW.

Huh. So Moff didn't just randomly add the TARDIS's invisibility feature for season 6. It's been there since...well...the original season 6.

I wonder if Travers was the Doctor's first recurring contact in the series. I know he won't show up here, but at least he's been mentioned.

Okay, so I'll admit I'm really not a big fan of Cosgrove Hall's animation, but they've been giving this scene a fascinating film noir tone.

Wow. I thought this story was supposed to take place on modern-day Earth, but they're making it sound almost like a dystopian future.

Of course, we're operating in UNIT-time at the moment...

Isobel! Nice to finally meet you! Having a little photoshoot, are we?

So the professor and his daughter have been replaced with another professor and his niece. I wonder if that was due to actor availability.

Okay InfoText, do your thing.

Ahhhh. It wasn't about availability, it was about the reduced importance of the character compared to the Yeti stories. That makes sense.

That's odd. It's Zoe's name always supposed to have those two dots above the "e"? (I know there's a name for that, but I can't remember it.)

There's a Lady Gaga "walk, walk, fashion baby" joke in here somewhere. For now, I'll just say "work it guuuurl."

Wait...is that animooted!Benton?

Hello, Tobias Vaughn! One of my followers speaks very highly of you.

Umm, Jamie, might I ask what was with that romantic-looking gaze you just threw at Packer even though he just tried to deck Two in the face?

"What is it?"
"Surely you've seen them about? They're disposable transistor radios."
JAMIE'S IPOD!

Oh wow. That image of Vaughn posing by the window would make an AWESOME desktop image.

"Script Editor: Terrance Dicks." Again, wow. That man's been around this show for a loooooong time.

They've been gone for "a couple of hours?" Isobel, were you on the floor that ENTIRE time?

I'm not sure what it is, but Zoe's hair looks a lot less shiny and a lot more fluffy in this story.

Patrick Troughton and Frazer Hines, I love you and everything you choose to be.

Umm, Isobel, again I have to ask: are you playing the Teddy Bear Picnic song for Zoe on a phonograph?

Ah, that WAS Benton in the car! And now they're on a plane, which should mean…

"How nice to see you again, Doctor."
"Colonel Lethbridge-Stewart!"
"Um, Brigadier now, I've moved up in the world."
#BRIIIIIIIIIG

Easily my favorite part of this is how the Brig is keeping a little smile during this whole conversation.

Even though the Brig is the classic military skeptic it's wonderful to see the hunk of joy he has at getting to meet this magical man again.

This is Zoe Herriot. She is wearing a feather boa in an office building. This fate could have been avoided if she had a Sassy Gay Fr…wait.

On the other hand, the girl knows how to work a computer. (I still don't quite get why they made Two so aggressively angry last episode.)

Well Vaughn, those are some lovely nostril shots of Two and Jamie's you've got there.

Wow, computers are pissing EVERYONE off in this story, aren't they?

How to Break a Computer: 1) Talk math to it. 2) Stand back while computer explodes. 3) Laugh.

("Initial publicity gave Zoe's age as fifteen, though this was never spelt out on screen.") And Now We Know.

Agh. I can't take my eyes off the Brigstache. It just looks so prominent and...*there*.

"Look, Jamie, sandwiches." I WILL NEVER BE ABLE TO WATCH THIS SCENE PROPERLY AND CERTAIN PEOPLE KNOW WHY.

alfhadlsfhdlskahfdslka Jamie pawing for his iPod...I mean, radio is probably one of the adorablest things ever.

Oh dear god. You know you're a little off when you turn on the InfoText and honestly expect it to mention that fanfic you co-wrote.

I was actually expecting Two to take the radio apart and find a tracking device in there instead of that other thing he found.

"A splendid little toy this is, Jamie."
"Ah, but it doesn't play tunes like mine."
It doesn't play tunes like mine. #doesntplaytuneslikemine

I also love how the Brig has made all these important (and accurate) observations about the Doctor just from one encounter.

Well, okay, so pretty much EVERYONE the Doctor meets remembers him, but the Brig seems to have a deeper understanding of how his mind works.

Meanwhile back at the Vaughn Cave, what exactly IS Planet 14? That can't be Mondas, can it?

"You forget *I* control the operation from Earth!" Wow. Like Chen before him, Vaughn will have none of his metallic partners' bullshit.

Has anyone else noticed that Vaughn seems to have one eyebrow cocked at all times? It looks like it's trimmed that way.

This episode is certainly letting a lot of panty shots slide through, isn't it?

A wild Jamie appears! Jamie uses Tackle! It's not very effective...

Speaking of which, wow, Frazer, those are some mightily toned calf muscles you've got there.

Have I mentioned yet how much I love the fact that part of Zoe's boa is sticking out of the cabinet?

If I didn't know better, I'd say Jamie's lips were pursed to emit a particularly unsavory word just now.

("This business was Frazer Hines' unscripted contribution.") How did I know it was going to say almost exactly that?

Also, I love how the InfoText almost never calls it "ad-libbing," it's always an "unscripted contribution."

So I've only just noticed, but is this the serial when Jamie finally lowers his socks? Or did he have them down in The Dominators? ...He did

Oh my god. Doctor Who predicted Apple.

This is Yet Another Patrick Troughton's Face Appreciation Post.

"He's being as nice as pie." New headcanon: Jamie likes pie.

And now we finally get to meet Professor Watkins! That's quite a beard you've got on you, sir.

Actually, you know who he almost reminds me of, appearance-wise? A short, balding Delgado!Master.

Also, I'm starting to see Packer as kind of an evil Benton.

...I just realized that I REALLY want to see Benton vs. Packer. That would be an AWESOME fight.

Effing magnets, how do they work? Well, Doctor + magnet = broken spy camera.

A surprising amount of escapes in this show succeed with the oh-look-behind-you tactic.

Stuck in an elevator together? CLING!

"Where does that lead?"

"Out into the lift shaft I imagine. Quickly, on me back."
"You know something?"
"Hm?"
"You're a clever wee chappie."

More Who Math: Two + Jamie = the best thing.

"Just been thinking: what happens if they get the lift going before we get to the top?"
"Oh that's simple: we get squashed."
"Wh-WHAT?!?"

Okay, is Packer talking to a chipmunk on the other end of that communicator?

I love how Vaughn's voice patterns stay basically the same but get louder and higher pitched when he's angry.

Smug Packer is smug.

"Kilroy was here." ("Kilroy wasn't there. The graffiti was a Troughton-Hines co-production.") OH MY GOD.

TROUGHTON + HINES = KILROY

In other news, our heroes escaped to the rooftop safely while temporarily reverting to puppies and clambering over each other.

("Frazer Hines was understandably sensitive about camera angles whenever Jamie had to climb anywhere.") #darknessunderthekilt

Ack. Never mind what I said about Vaughn a few minutes ago. He's pretty legit angry now.

And so Jamie finds himself trapped in a confined space with a strange man. #nocomment

Meanwhile, back in animated-land...
Hmm. Vaughn seems convinced that emotions can help defeat "their allies." I have a feeling he's not too far off.

It amuses me how the Brig refers to Jamie as "the boy" but he calls the pilot "Jimmy."

"Don't look now, but we're being spied on." You could just say "watched."

Ah, here we are, the famous helicopter rope ladder scene!

Out the window and up the ladder...oh wait now we have people with guns...

("Frazer Hines realized that the helicopter updraft was going to be a problem, even though he wore football shorts under his kilt.")

AHA! MYSTERY SOLVED.

And yet Isobel still gets an animated panty-shot. Was that really necessary, guys?

Yikes. Says a lot about Vaughn's influence that he can just ring up the Ministry of Defense on speed-dial like that.

So now, nearly 3 episodes later, they're finally returning to the issue of that attack at the very beginning of the story.

"Brigadier, you don't by any chance know where I can find a canoe?" Suddenly, CANOE. (Wait, I thought this footage survived.)

Huh. According to the InfoText, the composer for this serial had a background in jazz. That explains the tone of the score here.

Actually, I was meaning to mention this a while ago, but I REALLY like the music for this serial.

This is the second time I've heard the Cybermen drum beat leitmotif snuck into the score...

...and there they are!

As much as I wasn't terribly fond of the animation, I think I'm actually going to miss those episodes in a way.

Ah, THERE'S our canoe footage.

Meanwhile back at UNIT, looks like Isobel's got an admirer :3

Wow. Rutledge's office was a lot more atmospheric in the animated version than in the original telecast. Kudos, Cosgrove.

The Brig reporting to a higher authority. Now there's something I don't see every day. Not gonna lie, it's kinda weird.

Hmm. I'm starting to wonder if Rutledge might actually be under Cyber control and not Vaughn's.

Oh, so it IS Vaughn's control, but it's starting to weaken.

Huh. I think this is the first time the Cybermen have had glowing panels on their chestplates (as opposed to non-glowing ones).

Jamie, you just willingly handed over your radio. Are you feeling alright?

The way that pipe was angled, I almost thought that Cyberman was bending down to sit on a toilet.

The Cybermen screams are having a weird effect on me. On one hand, I kinda feel bad for it. On the other hand, OH GOD THAT NOISE.

The Brig does not understand Isobel's camera jargon. Relax, Brig, it's just the photo version of Doing Science To It.

But enough about Cybermen, let's talk about feminism! #wellthatwasrandom

"Well just because you're a man, you think you're superior, do you?" "Now I didn't say that. 'Course it's true..."

Jamie, if you didn't have the Product Of His Environment tag attached to you, I'm afraid a few smacks would be in order right about now.

Ah, so the boss in charge is called the "Cyber-Director" this time, apparently. Why do they keep changing that?

"No! My body may be cybernetic, but my mind stays human!" OH. OKAY. THIS IS NEW.

Looks like they're having a little trouble with that massive sliding door prop. Not moving quite so smoothly, is it?

I'm a little more amused than I should be at the Brig's use of the phrase "those crazy kids" to describe Jamie, Zoe, and Isobel.

Benton! So *you* were the unwitting transport in "those crazy kids'" shenanigans.

Funny that the script should leave Benton's character as anonymous when his name is clearly stated multiple times.

Although it seems that Benton's usual role is taken by Sergeant Walters in this story. Did Two call Benton a corporal in The Three Doctors?

I wonder if this trek through the sewers was something like what The Web of Fear originally was before it got burninated.

Wow. That cop's got quite a 'stache on him.

Annnnnnnd now he's dead. Oh well, I guess only the Brigstache is allowed to survive in this story.

"It's out of control. It's sort of wild!" A wild Cyberman appeared! What will Jamie do? Pokemon / Ball / Item / Run

Ooo, they've got good cybervoices this time!

Wow. That Cyberman standing up from the grenade blast might be the single most human movement I've ever seen a Cyberman do.

Jamie, I understand your intentions but maybe holding off on the UNIT folk finding you for another few minutes wasn't such a good idea.

I love how the music is so casual and paced and then oh beeteedubbs there's a Cyberman grabbing Jamie's leg, FYI.

UM. HEY GUYS. I THINK PUTTING THE MANHOLE COVER BACK ON MIGHT BE ADVISABLE.

Ah, THERE'S Two's Science Eyebrows.

So after all that danger to get the photos of the Cybermen, Brig says "no, you fail." Thanks. Thanks a lot.

Oh my god Vaughn you psychotic devious monster, you.

"Vaughn, obviously I can't choose but work for you. If I refuse, you'll torture me, or kill me. Now, I can't stand up to torture...I don't want to die, and you're an evil man, Vaughn. You're sadistic, you're a megalomaniac, you're insane...I pity you...but if I get half a chance...I'LL KILL YOU."

A lot of it's in the delivery, but DAYUM. And people say there weren't as many amazing speeches in Classic Who.

And now Vaughn is willingly giving him Packer's gun and putting it in Professor Watkins' hand. I have no words anymore.

AND HE BITCHSLAPPED HIM FOR NOT SHOOTING AND THEN HE SHOT HIM AND VAUGHN IS BULLETPROOF AND OH MY GOD THIS SCENE.

Cut back to Two Doing Science To It and Jamie being too adorable.

Wow. They skipped the whole rescue of Professor Watkins to cut right to one of Vaughn's lackeys giving him the bad news? Odd.

Random observation: the Brig really isn't that tall, is he?

I love how Jamie's seen the Cybermen so many times by now that his reaction to the situation is to go back to sleep.

Also, Zoe. I do not understand how your face works. Or your eyes. What are your eyes even.

("Kevin Stoney's permanently arched eyebrow and squint were the result of a serious facial injury earlier in his life.") And now I know.

I know I'd mentioned the eyebrow earlier, but he's got one full eye closed in this scene for some reason.

Aww. I was hoping they'd explain what the injury actually was.

Hey, Zoe's got her sparkly catsuit back on OH CRAP THE INVASION IS STARTING.

Also, is it just me, or does Two's position on the floor here seem reminiscent of One right before his regeneration?

And can someone explain to me the need for Cybermen to have shoelaces?

So I imagine that the Cybermen's control noise was terrifying back then, but now it's really annoying and I want it to stop.

The world becomes his, and Vaughn just sits there reading a book. Or playing with an iPad or something.

Oh. It's just a regular clipboard. Never mind.

So I only just realized: probably because of Stoney's facial tics, they almost never film him from the angle that shows it.

Oh crap drastic escape and OH DEAR GOD DID JAMIE JUST GET SHOT.

So all this time I thought that Jimmy and Sergeant Walters were the same person. Apparently they aren't.

"Seems to be a total blanket all over the world." I have to admit that would be a lot more threatening-sounding if we could actually see it.

Although I'm glad they at least had those shots of the random people on the street hearing the cyber-control.

Possible solution for saving the world from cyber-invasion: hijack the Russians.

Good, Jamie's situation is "just a small flesh wound" so Frazer Hines can take a holiday.

It both amuses and annoys me that the Brig keeps pronouncing "Cybermen" like "Cybemun."

For me, watching any Doctor other than Three drive a car is a little weird, but with Two it's just adorable. Especially with this music.

Also, the contrast of little Zoe in her shiny sparkle suit and her frowny face amongst all the big official UNIT men is just as adorable.

Creepier adorableness: Vaughn happily swiveling around in his chair. Also, LOVE Packer's exasperated eyeroll in response.

("How do dress your Cyberman, in seven easy stages.") ...I bow down before whoever wrote the InfoText.

Pat, your whispering voice could very easily be used for seduction purposes. Please use this power for good and not for evil.

("Your full-dressed Cyberman is now ready to conquer the world!") #omg #this #forever

So, my lovely Brit followers, I have to ask: do you folks all pronounce the letter Z as "zed?" Or that just a regional thing?

Something about this scene is making Patrick Troughton look taller as Two gets the upper hand on Vaughn. I am very impressed by this.

Meanwhile in Russia... (oh dear god why are that one guy's eyes still open and staring unblinkingly at that other guy)

Oh wait, never mind, this scene isn't in Russia.

Zoe's chain-reaction-explosion theory resonates with me more than it should thanks to how much Angry Birds I've played this week.

And now it's time for another edition of Zoe Herriot Blows Things Up With Her Brain.

("Wendy Padbury was an especially popular cast member with the extras.") Gee, I can't imagine why.#thatoneguyjustlookedatherglitter bum

"You'd better be right."
"I am!"

Aaaaaand boom goes the Cyberfleet.

Ah, never mind what I said earlier, they're filming Vaughn from

Stoney's poor side now. (Makes sense, now that his plan's falling apart.)

"IS THIS WHAT YOU WANTED? TO BE THE RULER OF A DEAD WORLD?" Interesting way to do a cliffhanger.

And now, at last, the epic conclusion.

Awww, Zoe's popular with the UNIT boys now :D

"Can't we keep her on, sir? She's much prettier than a computer!" Now THAT would've been an interesting way for Zoe to leave the show.

Well, that didn't exactly "blow them all sky high," but it certainly blew up the Cyber-director.

"Packer! Packer, where are you?" ...CYBERMAN. (Oh wow, that was actually really scary.)

And now it looks like Packer's finally gone. That sucks, he was quite a good henchman.

"Appealing to my better nature...no. If I help you, it'll be because I hate them. The Cybermen, my allies. You think I'm mad? That all I want is power for its own sake? No, I have to have power...the world is weak, vulnerable, a mess of uncoordinated and impossible ideals! It needs a strong man, a single mind, a leader..."
"VAUGHN! WILL YOU *LISTEN*???"
"...Right! I'll help you to destroy them because I hate them! They... destroyed...my dream..."

Oh. My. God. First of all, that was AMAZING. Second, I can actually see a tear forming at the edge of Vaughn's bad eye. #alltheawards

Aww, part of the reason we got Benton was that Douglas Camfield took a shine to John Levene. Result? Lots of close-ups in this episode.

Judging by this scenery, I'm guessing we're coming up on my favorite Patrick-Troughton-running sequence ever.

I love how UNIT gets a nice uppity military leitmotif in these past couple episodes.

Also, seeing Vaughn finally getting out of his office and running around instead of strutting is quite a fun treat.

Oh wow. Apparently Camfield was so intent on military authenticity that he got actual soldiers to play UNIT extras in this battle.

HERE IT IS. See Pat. See Pat Run. Run Pat, Run!

To Dodge a Bazooka: lay flat on the ground with your hands on your head and your feet in the air.

So the control tower for the bomb is destroyed off-screen, Vaughn might be dead, and we still have 8 minutes left. A bit anti-climactic, eh?

Well, okay, I know we still have the rest of the Cybermen to deal with...

"Yes, well this is going to be a long twelve minutes." Brig, have I mentioned recently that I love you?

And then there was a s'plosion! I can only assume that the danger's passed now that Isobel has Zoe posing for her photos again.

Oh god. This last scene. Find The Invisible TARDIS.

Wow. Benton got quite a high billing in the credits this time.

So they never really did explain how they got rid of the rest of the Cybermen all over the world, did they? Oh well...

So, all in all, that was a remarkably solid story considering its length!

Originally Posted July 8th, 2011

THE KROTONS

Written by Robert Holmes
Aired: December 28, 1968 – January 18, 1969

Wow. Less than 2 minutes in and we've already got a jealous-romantic subplot happening.

TWO!!! JAMIE!!! ZOE!!! HOLY CRAP I MISSED YOU GUYS!!!

And Two baritone-whistles along the rock quarry with an umbrella. Why am I automatically in love with this image.

That town is made of swiss cheese wedges. It...it seriously is.

Vaporized by...VAPOR! WHAT A CONCEPT!

"We are friends!" *instantly confronted by a crapton of spears*

"You wouldn't be so tough without these guards around you!"
"I accept your challenge!"
It is can be badass!Jamie tiems nao?

Holy...YES. YES IT WAS. A WINNER IS YOU. (And Two tries to shield himself and Zoe with his umbrella. HAH.)

"Doctor, what have they DONE to her?"
Two ignores and looks mournfully at now-destroyed umbrella "...the vandals..."

"I'm not a doctor of medicine, Zoe." ...well well well, this is certainly new...

Wait. Four's hypno-watch started with Two?

And Jamie actually DOES wear a watch! Fanart makes you aware of some strange things.

A large X appearing on a bleeping screen. I can actually imagine that being quite scary back in the day.

Oh, hang on, Mysterious Unseen Voice. That would be scarier.

"Now if this were an atomic laser, it might be more use!"
"An atomic laser? Is that better than an axe?"

Hey! It's the eyestalks from War of the Worlds!

I have to admit, I'm very amused by the way Jamie is clinging to Zoe when she's a good half-foot shorter than him.

"Hold out your hand, Jamie."
"What for?"
completely shameless slash radar going off

"Zoe, watch him. You know what he's like." D'awww...

"Yes, well, Zoe IS something of a genius. It can be very irritating at times."

So The Machine is actually alive? Also: "great jumping gobstoppers what was that." Two, I love you.

Hello, mysterious unexplained fishtanks?

Unexplained fishtanks have been explained. They appear to be...a primordial soup for robots?

Awww, heroic!Jamie thinks he can take on metal monsters with a crowbar. That's just adorable...

The Krotons

Wait, so the machine will kill Jamie with his own lack of intelligence? Also, do the Krotons have to narrate EVERYTHING they see?

Jamie shall be spared. YAY. Also, should I wonder out loud why Zoe's wearing such a short skirt? Or would that be a stupid question?

Wait what's with the mysterious floating salad bowls.

Does it puzzle anyone else that the Krotons have said repeatedly that Jamie "has no value," yet they're not really doing anything to him?

So Jamie prepares to bomb a Kroton while getting it to explain its weakness to him. That is quite impressive.

"Oh my giddy aunt." FINALLY. I'VE BEEN WAITING FOR HIM TO SAY THAT FOR A WHILE. *happy face*

I'd say Jamie just whipped out a literal can of whoop-ass.

Oh you fuckers did NOT just vaporize the TARDIS...

...actually, no they didn't! Clever Doctor and his emergency dematerialization system.

Two has been rock'd. This can't be good.

"Can I borrow your braces?"
"Noooo!"
Um, Zoe, general rule of thumb: do not mess with the Doctor's outfit. Ever.

Wait, maybe it's just because this is in black-and-white, but...is that rock BLEEDING?

"Jamie! I'd forgotten all about him in the excitement!" Shame on you, Two. Shame. SHAME.

Poor Jamie. He's been held captive, nearly mind-melted, and half-crushed by a door, and Two's STILL sending him off on errands.

157

Having never gotten to work in a lab in High School, I honestly have no idea what the sulfuric acid they're making will actually do.

And then there was a s'plosion!

So the Krotons basically just want to go home? I'll be interested to see where this goes.

The Second Doctor: Grand master of comical delay tactics. Patrick Troughton is one of my favorite people on this show for a reason.

Meltinggggggg...MELTINGGGGGGGG...

A chemistry lesson from the good folks at the BBC. Don't try this at home, kids.

Originally Posted April 24th, 2010

THE SEEDS OF DEATH

Written by Brian Hayles and Terrance Dicks
Aired: January 15 – March 1, 1969

Ah yes, this story got its own special title sequence. Don't think I've seen that since The War Machines.

I don't know how that monotone computer voice doesn't drive them all nuts after a while.

They keep using the term "Moonbase." I wonder if this is the future or the past of the one we see in, well, The Moonbase.

Ice Warrior POV! Wow, their voices are a lot different this time.

sigh When will fiction learn that "infallible" and "indestructible" really mean "marked for death?"

Wow. And it isn't until 8 minutes into the episode that we finally get to see our TARDIS crew.

"We're in a museum! A space museum!" Uh oh. Doctor, I hope you remember what happened the LAST time you landed in one of those.

Ah, Fewsham, ya damn coward.

"You're wrong. There IS just one man, one man alone who can help us now." The Doctor...!...oh...you mean that other guy.

Ah yes, good ol' Future of Space Travel According to the 1960s.

Well, at least Eldred's not pointing guns at them anymore.

"How would they get beyond the moon?"
"Nobody cares anymore about exploring space!"
Poignant words just after the last Space Shuttle launch

You know, when dealing with a reluctant old scientist, it might be a good idea to *actually tell him the whole truth.*

Aww, rehearsal for this story was when the announcement of Pat's departure came out.

"I'm afraid the TARDIS is not suited to short-range travel." Don't worry, Doctor, it will be eventually.

Wait. What. There's a robot in the background that looks suspiciously like a creepy version of Rosie from The Jetsons.

Not sure if I noticed this the first time, but this is a great cautionary tale of the world's over-reliance on technology.

Of course, something like that would probably be more relevant in today's iWorld than back then. *caresses iPod and MacBook lovingly*

And that one guy somehow managed to evade Ice Warrior detection...how? Seriously, he's just hiding in plain sight.

technobabble technobabble technobabble technobabble

Ho boy, Jamie's getting ready for his first experience in "antiquated" space travel.

Obligatory Everything Goes Wrong Scene.

Meanwhile on the Moon, SCIENCE.

Oh well, I guess you couldn't boil an Ice Warrior and eat it lobster-style. It'd just melt.

"Whatever you do, keep transmitting!" Aaaaaand cue the transmitter burning out.

And now it's replaced in the same minute. Crisis averted?

("Frazer Hines somehow manages to get his hands stuck between Wendy Padbury's legs!!") Gee, I wonder how that could've happened...

I wonder what the laces on Jamie's sleeves were supposed to be for. I'd image they've gotten in the way or something.

Hah! I love how the music completely cuts out when Phipps pops up.

Wait. I know this is a weird thing to be noticing right now but, I don't seem to remember Pat having sideburns.

Ah, my commentary's all caught up now!

But before I sign off, I just want to say: This is a Patrick Troughton's Running Style Appreciation Post.

And also
"YOUR LEADER'LL BE ANGRY IF YOU KILL ME. I...I'm a genius!"
"Geeeeeniuuuuusssssssssssss..."

Woah wait where did that random hall of mirrors come from. TWENTY TROUGHTONS!

I think that's the first Classic example I've seen of "RUN!" followed by an extended sequence of...well...running.

Also, I love Two's running style for some reason.

OH NO EXPLODING PUFFBALL KNOCKED OUT THE DOCTOR WHAT

"That is unusual. Most humans would be dead." Well, guess what? HE'S A TIME LORD, MUTHAFUCKA.

OH SHIT NOT ZOE.

Yay, Zoe's okay! Also, DOCTOR THIS IS ACTUALLY A VERY INCONVENIENT TIME TO BE NOISILY REGAINING CONSCIOUSNESS.

Dammit, Fewsham, and just when I was starting to regain faith in you as a character...

So the Doctor didn't try to reverse the polarity of the fungus' neutron flow. He just frantically poured random chemicals on it. Nice.

WATER. I had a funny feeling...

WAIT NEVER MIND FEWSHAM'S STILL GOT A FEW TRICKS UP HIS SLEEVE.

Heroic Sacrifice. As expected.

OH I GET IT now Two can't get in to rescue them. THAT'S what the door-closing was about.

OH SHIT HE'S LEGIT TRAPPED NOW

"Oh my word, that was a dangerous situation!" Ladies and gentlemen, The Second Doctor: Time Lord of Understatements.

Ahahahahaha, Two looks like he's covered in snow...

Okay, Two's portable solar "ray-gun" is easily the funniest awesome thing I've seen in the Classics so far.

Wow. Even back then, the Doctor needed his companions to save him every few episodes.

Two's acting surprisingly chill about the whole "I'm trapped on the moon alone with Ice Warriors who want to kill me" thing...

Because this commentary happened in my earliest days of live-blogging, I didn't do the entire serial in order. The first section of this commentary was posted on July 10th, 2011, with the later half posted on February 3rd, 2010

THE SPACE PIRATES

Written by Robert Holmes
Aired: March 8 – April 12, 1969

Wow. Less than a minute in and we've already got one ship taking a docking bay roughly from behind.

Also, I don't think we've had our title card yet.

Oh, never mind, there it is. Also, s'plosion! And Robert Holmes!

Most Valuable Mineral/Substance of the Week: Argonite.

Wait, did the general just say that one guy's name was Ian?

Meanwhile in Space, more hot steamy ship-on-beacon action.

For some reason, Caven's suit (especially the helmet) kinda reminds me of Sark's outfit in the original Tron.

Just like Seeds of Death: 10 minutes in and still no sign of the TARDIS or its inhabitants.

Well, okay, I guess that's kinda close: they're approaching a planet called Ta. Now all they need to do is go to Rd and Is.

THERE'S the TARDIS! And considering the instructions we just heard, this is going to follow the usual wrong-place-at-the-wrong-time plot.

Jamie, if you don't mind me saying, you look like you just walked off the set of Treasure Island or something. I think it's the shirt.

"There's only one thing we can do."
"What?"
"Run!"
As is to be expected.

SURPRIIIIIIISE!

Oh. Well at least that misunderstanding got sorted out right away. Although it probably could've ended with fewer people dying.

"I am going to get that gang of murdering thieves if I have to spend the next ten years out here!" Theeeeeere we go.

By the way, they sure are having fun with the music in this serial, aren't they?

Ah yes, we appear to be approaching the famous oxygen-deprivation scene...

You know, seeing it properly now, the pirate ship design kinda looks like a precursor to the concord jet. Unless they existed already...

That choral music over the titles...I KNOW I've heard that somewhere before. The Ice Warriors, perhaps?

"Ah, coffee!" Coffee! It solves all our problems!

Meanwhile, onboard the plaid-patterned block in the perfectly organized and evenly spaced field of debris...

Huh. I'm starting to wonder if that mysterious stalled ship is actually the TARDIS floating around in space.

Oh, never mind, it's just...a rocket...piloted by a chair with a jacket on...with a control panel that lays eggs...

THERE'S the captain. And he's singing Somewhere Over the Rainbow. Spare a little context anytime soon?

"Rubbishy newfangled solar toasters..." Okay...we now return to: Hillbillies in Space.

No really, he's got the gingham check shirt, the neckerchief, the accent, the disdain for technology...am I watching the same show?

Apparently the chap's name is Milo Clancey. Actually, he sounds way too American to be called a "chap," though.

Ah. Nearly 8 minutes in and we FINALLY return to our heroes.

And they cut away right before Jamie gets sprayed in the face with something :/

Milo even says "howdy." Usually I find these oddities funny but they're taking everything else so seriously that it just feels out of place.

I'm starting to wonder if these people aren't really human, because they never say "Earth," just "home planet."

Okay. Seriously. We're halfway through the episode and we've had about a full minute of Team Two. What the balls.

Ah, there they are! I feel like I'm watching the right show again.

Oh wow, they actually explained why the debris exploded so evenly. Also, Zoe, those are literally the shortest short-shorts I've ever seen.

"I would've put him through the mind probe, sir." All together now... NO, NOT THE MIND PROBE!

"What's he doing now?"
"I have no idea. Ask him."
"What's the use? He's got his *mysteeeerious* face on."

...ohcrap. That Jamie-tongue screencap I thought was so adorable all this time was actually him realizing that their oxygen was running out.

Also, why is that guy wearing an Ice Warrior helmet?

Oh wait, sorry, that's an Ice LORD helmet. Also, only in this scenario can we hear the phrase "oh Doctor, can we have some more oxygen?"

Although on second thought, there's probably a LOT of uses for that phrase.

Jamie's face: Effing magnets, how do they work? #miraclesman

I could've sworn Two just said "electromagnetic pie" instead of "electromagnetic power."

"Zoe, don't be such a pessimist." Wow. It touches my heart a little how that sounded a little more like a plea than an offhanded request.

We now appear to be on the planet Ta, where the women appear to have large metal bathing caps instead of hair.

This would be an opportune moment for some reversal of the polarity. Unfortunately, everything in general seems to be going to shit.

"Madam, you'd need a 90M computer to work that out!" If that means "ninety megabyte," I will be thoroughly amused.

Aww, they're all lying together...waiting to die...oh wait they're being rescued OH GOD THEY SHOT JAMIE

Ugh. I am seriously getting sick of these scenes with the space patrollers.

GHAAAA. WHY DON'T THE GENERAL'S EYES LOOK REAL IN THIS SHOT. #uncannyvalley

"A boy, a girl, and a nutcase! You can't be the pirates!" Trust me, nutcases can be pirates. Let me introduce you to Captain Jack Sparrow...

Milo's voice is starting to sound even more like a mix of American Southern and British.

A china teapot is smashed to pieces? OH NOES, NOT THE TEAPOT! We only knew it for about five seconds...

Wait. If argonite is "used for everything," then how is it so expensive? Wouldn't the law of supply and demand make it cheaper?

Or maybe I just made a major economics fail, I don't know.

There's an "I've got 99 problems but a _____ ain't one" joke in here somewhere...

Ah yes, good ol' Cassette Tapes in the Future.

Um, hello, why is Seventies Porn Colin on that communications monitor?

Poor Doctor. Finding the TARDIS again overrides everything.

And now Zoe Herriot presents: Math and Science.

So I wonder if these two pirates are supposed to be the Holmes Double-Act.

I know this goes without saying but, those are surprisingly well-lit tunnels.

Well, looks like they've found the pirates' blast furnace, or at least the prep room for it.

Come on, guys, this is no time to go spelunking.

Patrick Troughton's worried-panic groans are more hilarious than worried-panic groans have any right to be. This man is wonderful.

"What are you carrying drawing pins for?"
"I LIKE drawing pins."

Jamie seems a tad prone to leg injuries this season, doesn't he?

Looks like argonite isn't the only thing the pirates are stealing. That guy on the communication screen has the Brigstache!

I think I just realized why the space patroller scenes bug me so much: so far, their mission has had the most indirect effect on Team Two.

In short: it feels like Holmes is writing THEM as the main characters and the TARDIS crew is just tacked on; otherwise it wouldn't be Who.

(Yes, I'm aware that Mission to the Unknown still counts as an episode despite having no TARDIS folk, because it's the Master Plan prequel.)

"Nothing disappears in space!" ARE YOU QUITE SERIOUS. ARE YOU AWARE OF HOW BIG SPACE IS. Where's my Hitchhiker's Guide...

"Space," it says, "is big. Really big. You just won't believe how vastly, hugely, mindbogglingly big it is." And there you go.

Ah, good ol' studio-made rock.

"Which end did ye land on when ye fell down that shaft?" Jamie, come on, you should know the Doctor's Science Puzzle Time when you see it.

On that note, if Pat was the inspiration for Davison's Doctor, I can see why he wanted to do more tech improv without the sonic screwdriver.

Okay, I take back my earlier comment about these guys being Human Aliens. It's perfectly plausible that they're just Humans of the Future.

In other words, like Leela: descendents of mankind that colonized and grew up on other planets.

That pirate guard looks suspiciously CGI-rendered. I guess there just weren't any images, video or telesnap, of them from that angle.

Come to think of it, this whole story doesn't have any telesnaps, does it?

What's with my sudden obsession with pointing out phallic spaceship imagery? (I swear, that ship just put a condom on.)

"Doctor, that noise! It's getting on everybody's nerves!" NO HANNAH DO NOT START SINGING THAT SONG

Jamie-Smash: the solution to all our problems.

Umm, Jamie...just like you don't bite the hand that feeds you, you don't bitch at the person who saved you from asphyxiating in space.

I cannot handle all these Texasisms on Doctor Who at once. (No offense to any of my followers from Texas.)

Slight slip-up: Jamie talks, but they show Two instead.

Caven has one of the creepiest smiles. Seriously. What.

Suddenly, INFODUMP.

Also, Jamie's getting a little trigger-happy. I hope that thing is set to Stun.

("...Jamie edges away in a crab-like shuffle.") Wait. BUT I WANT TO SEE THAT.

Like Caves of Androzani, I'm not sure who's on who's side anymore. And I care less. (In Caves I actually WANTED to know.)

I'm sorry if I'm treating this story with an unusual amount of vitriol, but maybe I'm just that ready to be done with the recons.

Either that, or I was expecting a lot more from a Robert Holmes story. Then again, this was only his second Who outing, wasn't it?

Continuing my groanings from last time, I think I officially stopped paying real attention to the patrol ship scenes a while ago.

Wait...the person in the portrait is supposed to be someone's mom? But that's a picture of a dude...

Oh wait, that was "father" not "mother." That's what I get for not listening with headphones on, I guess.

And Zoe doesn't know how candles work. Well, I guess it's the same kind of technology gap as me not knowing how to use a printing press.

(By which I mean, the kind where you have to set the type letter by letter and everything.)

Also, finally a mention of Earth. I guess that puts that debate to rest.

Also also, the plot is finally starting to thicken! Mysterious Victorian room in space and a frightened old man hiding under a table...

I might've just heard this wrong, but I could've sworn Milo just said, "don't you know me, dawg?"

I did. The guy's name is Dom.

Wow. For something that had been just a wild goose chase story up until now, this scene is surprisingly emotional.

Awwww, old space chums reunited.

Remember back when I thought that this serial was only 4 episodes long? I stand by that. At least the pace is starting to pick up now.

I didn't think I'd say this, but now that this is turning into more of a complex human drama I might just need to give this a re-listen.

Caven is becoming a lot like Tom Baker: there aren't many ways he can smile that aren't horribly creepy.

Wait. Madeline's father's been kept in that room near her headquarters while she thought he was dead. What.

Yikes. It's kinda sad to see her completely breaking down like this after she'd shown herself to be a relatively strong woman before.

"You know, Jamie, sometimes I think you don't appreciate all I do for you." DDDDD:

Uh oh, looks like Caven did something to Madeline while the communications were cut...

Wait, when did Two get separated from Jamie and Zoe?

LAST. RECON. EPISODE. AT LAST.

"Oh, don't touch him, Jamie! Don't touch him at all!" That might be a bit much to ask, Zoe. #CLING

This seems to be a rare protagonist occurrence of Break The Haughty.

"They're not there!"
"THENWHEREARETHEY?!?!?"
#suddenlyLOUD

Wow. That was a surprisingly smooth set of images.

"I think that's the air conditioning circuit reconnected." Well, at least they'll be cool. It's pretty hot out there in space.

(For anyone wondering, yes part of that joke came from the fact that I'm caught up in the Eastern US heatwave right now.)

Again: some physical comedy and we don't get to see it.

It's probably the accent, but I keep hearing Milo pronouncing Dom's name like "dawg." I'm okay with this.

Time seems to be traveling at a rate of about 4 minutes a minute right now.

Six minutes to stop a nuke, six minutes left in the episode. NOW we're back in real time. In a manner of speaking.

("It now reads 11:55.") Except it doesn't. ...Ah, there we go.

Hellooooo, is that surviving footage I just saw?

("The missiles make contact and the pirate ship is blown to pieces!") YAAAAAY.

I really wish I could see this ending for real. It's a surprisingly touching scene with music to match.

And with just over a minute left, we return to one of our original conundrums: how do we get the TARDIS back?

Well that answers that. And everyone goes out laughing! Awwww.

Okay. Now. I finally get to say: I. AM. DONE. WITH. RECONS. FOREVER! ...I'm actually just a little sad about it. End of an era.

Originally Posted July 24th, 2011

THE WAR GAMES

Written by Malcolm Hulke and Terrance Dicks
Aired: April 19 – June 21, 1969

The beginning of the end, and it opens with SO MANY RAPID S'PLOSIONS.

Small, innocent, unassuming TARDIS crew, stepping out into mud and laughing... ;___;

Hello...unexpected explorer woman? You seem frighteningly okay with the whole being-stranded-out-in-no-man's-land thing.

Ohhhhh, I see, it's a medical van.

Maybe it's just from seeing Blackadder Goes Forth and War Horse but there's something so much more raw about seeing the team in World War I.

Like, there's a much stronger feeling of them being out of their element. The TARDIS can't help them here because IT'S FRIGGING WORLD WAR I.

So naturally they mention a General Smythe and all I can think of is Evelyn.

"5,000 specimens." Aaaaand there's our first tip-off that something sci-fi is going on here.

173

It never surprises me at this point when some odd action happens between Two and Jamie it comes up as "unscripted business" in the InfoText.

Symthe's glasses seem to have special hypnotic powers. That's...highly disturbing.

Also, I can't help looking at Barrington and thinking "oh my god, it's Blackadder played straight." #peoplewholooklikerowanatkinson

This scene is turning into quite a dark foreshadowing of how this serial is eventually going to end...

N'aaaaaawwwww, but Two loves his Zoe.

Sneaky Zoe is sneaky.

So I wonder if the first episode of Caves of Androzani borrowed from this: mockery of justice and a cliffhanger with a firing squad.

Two conveniently saved by some other guy getting shot. And Zoe seems to have no qualms about climbing over dead bodies.

Now that sounds familiar...AH YES. A TARDIS IN ITS NATURAL STATE.

"What year do ye think i' is?"
"Year? Why, it's 1745!"
DUN DUN DUUUN.

Ahhhh, THIS must be where Two pretends to be a prison inspector. Poor baffled soldier.

James Robert McCrimmon is going to fuck your shit up with a stick and dramatic music.

"Civilians? Well, tell them to wait! I'm having my tea." #tea #thesolutiontoeverything

Yikes. Two is taking this role with a METRIC CRAPTON of gusto.

Jeebus. When Ten said that the monsters had nightmares about him, clearly the monsters had met prison-inspector-Two.

Well, considering Two and the redcoat just made their escape on their own, I get the uncomfortable feeling that Two's plan is rendered moot.

Oh, never mind, they know about it now.

Prison warden threatening to report you and your time traveling friends? Smash them over the head with a vase of pretty flowers.

I wonder if this is our first glimpse of Time Lord perception filter technology.

Hang on, there's that weird mist everyone was talking about...well, at least they're not near the front lines anymore.

Looks like they're still in modern times, what with the paved road and fences.

Oh wait, never mind. INCOMING ROMANS!

Attacked by Romans? Just switch into Reverse to go forward in time. Because that makes perfect sense.

Also, yikes, Two, that's quite a rip you've got in your trousers.

Apparently all they have to do is mention going somewhere to find a map to suddenly make this sound like a fantasy RPG.

"Jamie, I wonder whether perhaps I can pick this lock."
"Aye, with a tuning fork?"
Pat. Your face.

Ahhhhhhh. And finally the sporran-folding comes into context.

Huh. I didn't think candle wax was that easily detachable from the wick.

Cool! I can make out other zones on the map! Let's see...British Civil War, Crimean War, Russo-Japanese War...and that's all I can read.

Sonic screwdriver's back! Now why couldn't he just've used that on the safe instead of going through all that bother with the bomb...

...oh right, timing. And other reasons.

And now we've got a hypno-monocle. Also, impressive that they're using actual German for some of their dialogue here.

Woah. Suddenly, FUTURE. Also, THE WAR CHIEF.

"They escaped my human lieutenant." Wait...HUMAN lieutenant? Are the hypno-leaders robots or aliens or something?

Huh. I think that's the first time we've actually heard someone's thoughts as a VO on this show.

Poor American soldiers, they've already fought the British twice and now they're getting their asses kicked by them in their own Civil War.

Good thing Carstairs' handgun seems to have unlimited ammo.

Another raw TARDIS! Let's have a look inside, shall we?

...Or it could just take off, leaving Jamie behind.

I just realized: this serial title sequence must've been murder for people with epilepsy. Because seriously that's a LOT of strobe lighting.

Time to play Judge the Quality of the American Accents. These aren't half bad so far.

Maybe it's because other Americans in 60's Who were from the South and West, but hearing normal American accents here almost sounds weird.

Okay, that was officially the most pitiful excuse for an outdoors backdrop ever. YOU CAN SEE THE CREASES IN THE PAPER WHERE IT FOLDS.

Aaaaaaand cue the Confederate soldiers with the distinct Southern accents.

Awww, that one guy was actually being quite a gentleman, but then HYPNO-MONOCLE.

Fun with visors!

Suddenly, rescued by random dude! Awesome.

AND HE'S IMMUNE TO THE HYPNO-MONOCLE. I bow to your badassery, sir.

Ahhhh, here's the clip that Frazer showed us in The Time-Traveling Scot where he was doing his best John Wayne.

("Riding a horse was not usually a challenge for Frazer Hines - but this time he had to do it wearing a kilt!") #pffffftttttt

("Afterwards he found that all the hair had rubbed off his inside legs. But there was some compensation: on the bus home he got a thigh massage from a make-up girl.")

And now we know almost exactly what's going on. Thank you, Mr. Exposition Man! And hello again, Carstairs!

Aaaaaand after being reprocessed, he immediately singles out Two and Zoe as German spies. Greeeat.

Meanwhile in America... (interesting choice of music for a chase scene)

ACTION-SCOT TO THE RESCUE! Or maybe not...

Two, I think I understand what you're trying to do, but perhaps drawing more attention to yourself like that isn't the best of ideas.

Not a good time to be recognizing old schoolmates either, it seems. That was easily the most desperate "RUN, ZOE, RUN!" I've heard from Two.

Carstairs is free again! Which, unfortunately, could turn out to be a major problem right about now.

Huh, looks like one of the rebels is from Jamie's time. He's got a kilt, anyway...

Aw, I was hoping we'd find out where Harper was from. I know his actor is from Trinidad, but I can't place the character's accent.

Of course...that could very well be a Trinidadian accent. Not sure I've ever heard one before.

Locking away Zoe in the swirly room for interrogation? Not sure that'll get you the answers you want to hear.

I get quite a hefty dollop of satisfaction seeing the bad guys using some kind of truth-forcing device and STILL not getting their answers.

So, I still don't understand why they keep referring to the first place as the 1917 Zone and not the World War I Zone.

(And it was 9:17 when I tweeted that. Huh.)

Poor Harper. He was quite a brave man. Well, at least the resistance folk know about the TARDISes now.

"Aye, well ye probably have to do something very special with them." #nocontextforyou

That last gesture seemed to imply some significance of the emblem the War Chief has around his neck. A Time Lord artifact, perhaps?

"Ah, Lady Jennifer, I don't think you should come."
"Because I'm a woman?"
"Ye...uh, no, uh...well, in a way, yes."
"That settles it, then, I'm certainly coming."
BAM.

Hmm, is this a possible snippet of affection for Carstairs I'm seeing here?

"But the War Chief...he's the only one who understands space-time travel!"
"And his people."

#TIEMLOARDS

There seem to be quite a few hearing impaired people in this serial if they keep missing all those whispers.

NO NO NO DON'T KILL JAMIE.

Nah, I know he lives, but it's never pleasant watching him gunned down. And with that we reach the half-way mark!

"Are you suggesting he's bringing in his own people? The Time Lords?" And that, unless I'm mistaken, must be their first named mention ever.

A vibe I've been getting from actually watching this as opposed to hearsay is that the War Chief answers to the Warlord and not vice versa.

Of course, the War Chief is the one I always hear about as this story's villain and I didn't even hear of the Warlord until recently...

So that's my defense. On with the show.

Suddenly, cloakroom.

(I'll bet the Doctor was one of those little boys that liked to run around and hide in coat racks in clothing stores.)

First Jamie looks dead-ish...but then you see his crossed ankles and then it looks like he's just laying there, chillin'.

We get a good instance of the Doctor using his techno wits to solve a problem but then Zoe comes out with "why don't you just sonic it?"

Okay, so she's just suggesting that they use it as a power source. Okay, that works.

Aww, close-up sleeping Jamie...wait. Guys, do we really need to be looking up his nostrils like that?

Ah, he seems to be waking up now. Hello again, shouty-War Chief!

Please tell me I'm not the only person who can't look at those walls without immediately thinking of the Cingular logo?

"I think you'll find that THAT piece goes in THERE."
"Ah, thank you!" *double-take*
lol u mad?

Meanwhile, back in the "Civil War"...

I honestly can't help but wonder what's up with the security chief's voice. Is it a character tic or just shoddy acting?

"Your first responsibility is to me!"
"No! My first responsibility is to the Warlord, and to my people."
So I guess it wasn't just a vibe.

...okay, I might just need a gif of Carstairs shooting that guy in the face. Because that was just badass.

You know, I keep hearing in certain places that Zoe's photographic memory is mentioned once but never used...but it sure comes up a lot.

NO NO NO DON'T GIVE HIM THE MONOCLE BACK HE'S GOING TO...too late.

Or maybe not? Ohhhhhh right, this soldier's in the resistance so he has a certain immunity to the hypno-glasses.

Wait a sec...what's that tape over his eye? I suspect that's to hold the monocle in place, but shouldn't it be on the other eye?

And more importantly, shouldn't you guys be...well...*not* zooming in on it like that?

Insert "are you my mummy" joke here. #gasmaskzombiesfrom1969

Oh sure, Two, that's a good idea. Just loudly announce your presence to the guards with guns who may not have noticed you yet.

...I'm trying so hard not to make a fellatio joke right now, you guys.

Guns are out, FISTFIGHT! We shall duel like MEN!

Hang on, there're other people still in the blank TARDIS, so why don't they just tackle the guy with the gun from behind or something?

Or shooting him, that works too. Nice shot, Moor.

I'm only just realizing how much I'd love a spin-off of the resistance. I'd really love to learn some of their stories.

Also, a band of soldiers from different times and cultures fighting together would just be excellent character exploration fodder.

That collapsing ceiling suddenly looks a lot less threatening now that we can see down through the holes in the top.

Ah, and there's the large white hanky of surrender.

Or it could be the large white hanky of HEY LOOK AT THIS SMOKE BOMB I'M THROWING ON THE FLOOR KTHXBAI

I remember from Neil Gaiman's old article that the blank TARDISes were called "SIDRATs," but I wasn't expecting the long "I" sound.

Yikes. The Warlord's glasses sure make his eyes look a lot bigger.

Aww, and just when we were starting to get happy-picnic music, suddenly ROMANS.

The time zone barriers look suspiciously like the white zone from the first episode of The Mind Robber...

Aaaaaaand now we're back in Smythe's office and everyone's going to be on the hunt for our heroes in the fake fields of France again.

Zoe! There you are!

It seems like we rarely see Two this consistently mad in any one scene, but the 1917 zone really brings out his bitter side, doesn't it?

Two facing a firing squad...I guess this counts as foreshadowing.

Clever Zoe covering up the camera. Also, satisfying to know that Smythe finally bit the dust.

I find it interesting that the War Chief is the more popular character when the Warlord is clearly in charge of everything.

And, for dorky reasons, I LOVE how Carstairs is speaking French to the French guy in a flat-out English accent.

turns on InfoText ...and it turns out the French guy is played by Michael Craze's younger brother. It's a small Whoniverse.

Two...why did you do that? Why did you run out in the open towards the guards just to save the machine? Now you've been captured.

It amuses me a bit more than it should that the cliffhanger ends on Jamie making a rather annoyed "well, shit" face.

Welcome to another edition of: Patrick Troughton Making High Whimpering Sounds When Something Bad Happens To Him.

...and usually when he concentrates, his face gets comically bunched up. But...not quite so this time.

Although I'm glad he figured out what no one else seemed to figure out about the interrogation machine: just keep your eyes closed.

I'm going to completely ignore the temporal grace debate that the use of that grenade brings up.

"Not you, Jamie."
"Aye?"
"Someone's gotta be in charge here."
"...Me?"
"Yes, lad. You."
"... :DD"

This is the first Time Lord vs. Time Lord face-off we've had since the Monk, isn't it? *gets front-row seats*

It's weird seeing this scene knowing, as a newer fan, that the Doctor as a runaway has been an established fact for years.

Well, okay he called himself an exile in Unearthly Child, but I think this is the first time his absence from Gallifrey is really discussed.

"My motives are purely peaceful." Riiiiiiiiiiiiiiiiiiiiiiight...

Meanwhile back at HQ, awwwwwwww Jamie...

I AM TRYING REALLY REALLY HARD HERE NOT TO MAKE A "NOBODY EXPECTS THE SPANISH INQUISITION" JOKE RIGHT NOW BECAUSE OH MY GOD.

(Okay yes I know they're from the Mexican Civil War like Zoe said but still you get the idea.)

Verdict: this man is a douche. Product of his environment, yes, but still a douche.

Also, completely random observation: Jamie must've switched to modern boots at some point. I don't think they made soles like that in 1746.

("As the performances developed, the friendly friction between [Jamie and Zoe] was complimented with an element of sexual tension.") WELP.

...Zoe how does draping Jamie in grenades help you at all I don't understand your plan.

I'm getting a little tired of that leitmotif. Also, I think that's the first time this story we've seen a Roman soldier in a studio shot.

More amused than I should be how the group at the base seem to be running this rebellion like a television pledge drive.

No really: they've got the jaunty music playing, the guys on the telephone, the map of all their successes...maybe more like an election.

I don't know about you guys, but something about this scene is screaming IT'S A TRAP!

Yyyyyyyyup. Which of course begs the question TWO WHAT ARE YOU DOING.

Ah, it always comes down to someone in power with the right knowledge wanting the Doctor's TARDIS, doesn't it?

I think I understand the fandom's theories about the War Chief being a pre-Master. He won't take his hand off Two's shoulder here.

Well, the resistance leaders have Two right where they want him. Maybe now the truth comes out...?

Okay, yes and no, I think. Baahh, everyone's too busy trying to violently murder Two.

On the other hand, clever boy Jamie for catching on and playing along.

Aww, and there's the knowing-wink. I wonder what war Zoe's going to pretend to be from?

I have to admit: between the War Chief and the security chief, I'm actually rooting for the former because I just hate the latter more.

I'm actually not saying I hate the War Chief; I love him, but the security chief is such a nasally slimeball. Great love-to-hate villain.

Oh, maybe the plan hasn't been compromised, but then where did the guards go...?

This is starting to feel like a reverse base-under-siege scenario. Also, War Chief offs security chief BAM that was satisfying!

"...the Time Lords."
"Well, who're they?"
"They're my own people, Jamie."
"Oh! Well that's alright, then!"
YOU. JUST. WAIT.

And there's the message box from The Doctor's Wife! #ivegotmail

And of course I remembered the answer to my question from a few nights ago: The War Chief is a Time Lord but the Warlord isn't.

I'm just going to assume the War Chief was on his last life or he got hit so badly he couldn't regenerate. Either way, ouch.

This sequence probably has the highest concentration of face-punching of any Doctor Who episode ever.

"Jamie...Zoe...this is where we say goodbye." NO YOU CAN'T, IT'S AN EPISODE TOO EARLY.

"...oh very well, but don't say I didn't warn you!" That's the spirit! Mostly...

Awwww, Carstairs wants to go back for Lady Jennifer! Please let them have a happy ending, since I know Team Two won't get one...

Well, at least he didn't get shot at the last second. Goodbye, Carstairs. I think you and Jennifer would've made great companions.

Okay, I know that last cliffhanger was supposed to be dramatic, but it came off as just really silly-looking. Still, the end draws nigh...

Alright Team Two...one last go, aye?

I wish I could quote this entire TARDIS scene, but that would take too long. Soooo gooooood though.

Hey, isn't that the same water-landing shot from Fury From the Deep? Oh hey fishies hello little fishies OH GOD SHARK.

And that was definitely the opening from The Web of Fear. You can even see the web!

Here we are: Gallifrey for the very first time. And the moment is ruined slightly by the clear view of the studio from the TARDIS doors.

Alrighty, let's see how Time Lord trials work sans the Valeyard growling at everything all the time.

There's a Care Bear Stare joke in here somewhere. But wow, I didn't think the Warlord had it in him to cower like that.

Suddenly GUARDS.

"Don't talk rubbish, of course he can steer it!" Ohohohoho, this'll be interesting.

Forcefield around their entire planet AND "it will be as if you had never existed?" Time Lords: Serious Business as always.

"I not only admit them, I am proud of them! While you have been content merely to observe the evil in the galaxy, I have been fighting against it!" But just the one galaxy, Doctor?

THAT FACE. I HAD NO IDEA THAT FACE WAS FROM THIS EPISODE. AND THIS SCENE, OF ALL MOMENTS.

Aww, Two and his cards. He's somehow gone from being terrified to being bored.

Sooooo, why exactly do the Time Lords need this misty swamp maze curtain thing in their trial building?

"There is no escape, Doctor. It is time to say goodbye to your friends." Nonononono...

"Well, goodbye Jamie."
"But...but Doctor surely we could..."
"...Goodbye, Jamie."
"I won't forget you, y'know?"
"Oh, I won't forget *you*!"
DDDDDD':

"They'll forget me, won't they?"
"Not entirely..."
Well, I have to admit, that's better than nothing. And then Tip of the Mind happens...

"I thought I'd forgotten something important, but it's nothing."
Making sad emoticons really isn't going to get me very far here.

"Tryin' to murder a McCrimmon, would ye? Well I'll show ye!" And after watching this bit with Frazer Hines, I can never take it seriously.

"You will be sent to Earth in the twentieth century, and will remain there for as long as we deem proper." Or, about three seasons.

"You can't just change what I look like without consulting me!!" Heeeere we go...

And as Brian Rimmer showed in one of his videos, all of Two's complaints show up in some incarnation or another of the Doctor.

"The time has come for you to change your appearance, Doctor, and begin your exile."

Jamie, Zoe, Pat, you three helped me find a love for Classic Who nearly 2 years ago when I was just starting out. Thank you for everything.

And with that, I complete not only the entire Second Doctor era, but the entire black/white era of Doctor Who. Yet another chapter closed.

Fortunately, the next chapter is one that I'm particularly looking forward to: color, Pertwee and, most importantly, Those UNIT Chaps!

Originally Posted October 12th, 2011

CHARACTER RETROSPECTIVE:
ZOE

Oh Zoe, you adorable little dollop of smart-sparkles. I can't help but adore any companion who can match wits with the Doctor, even if it makes him a little exasperated. Back when I wrote about the women of Doctor Who for school, I placed Zoe in the "Kids" category because I felt that she was defined more by her youth than by her brains. Not sure why I did that, since I specified at the start that she could "easily fit in the Intellectuals category." Really, she's both: she is young and smart.

One of the things I appreciate the most about her representation as a female teen genius is that no one ever asked her to trade her brains for being feminine and sociable. While she did have co-workers in The Wheel in Space who criticized her for being an emotionless little computer, she never has to choose between the two. She said she wanted to feel things "as well." Zoe wants to be both, and she gets to be both.

Having grown up with a lot of "makeover" movies in the '90s where the mousy bookish girl is made "hot" so she can attract boys, I found Zoe's arc to be a refreshing one. More importantly, she's allowed to develop friendships with other women. I feel like the contrast between her interactions with her co-workers on the Wheel and her escapades with Isobel in The Invasion is a perfect example of how much she grows during her time in the TARDIS. She gets to play fashion model *and* blow up a computer by outsmarting it.

Unlike Victoria before her, Zoe has a somewhat more conflict-driven relationship with Jamie. Not in the sense that they didn't like each other, but Jamie and Victoria were a complimentary relationship, whereas Jamie and Zoe are perfect foils for each other. She's the futuristic brains, he's the old-fashioned brawn. She's the Head, he's the Heart. It was fun watching them butt heads over their differences but still work towards the same goals of ultimately saving the day. Zoe is very much a young lady of the future, and probably would have agreed with Vicki's remark about The Beatles playing "classical music." Although somehow I doubt that her sparkly catsuit will come into fashion by her designated time of origin.

CHARACTER RETROSPECTIVE: JAMIE

I would just like to take this moment to apologize for the high num-ber of Jamie-related in-jokes that undoubtedly cropped up over the course of this book. ...Okay, now that I've got that out of the way, James Robert McCrimmon. I can't think of many other Classic com-panions who are loved so purely by fandom. If anyone could be said to be THE Second Doctor companion, it would be Jamie, in both the quantity and quality sense. He's a great, fun, nigh-on perfect character. Like Leela later, Jamie's fish-out-of-water sensibilities are put to both the uses of comedy and character development. We get moments of him gazing quizzically at things like magnets and computers and run-ning away from airplanes, but we also have him blending in perfectly with several different futuristic guard units and ultimately never letting his lack of understanding of technology get in the way of what was most important. Jamie asks questions. He learns. He's not "stupid" or "simple," he's just from another time. He puts loyalty first.

Then there's his relationship with the Second Doctor, which really is akin to an old married couple after a certain point. They bicker, they synchronize, they give each other admiring glances, and they cling to each other. A lot. Sometimes I do stop to wonder why exactly this dynamic works so well. Why this particular Doctor and this particular companion? Two isn't the "old man" that One was, as much as his companions might joke about it, and Jamie doesn't necessarily need to do all the heavy lifting (especially in their first season when Ben's around). So what's the secret? Really, I think it comes down to the actors. Virtually every behind-the-scenes chat with Frazer Hines I've seen shows just how strong his friendship with Patrick Troughton was, and how much they threw themselves headfirst into everything on the show. Easily my favorite on-set prank stories all come from Frazer or Pat deciding to get up to some shenanigans or another (I still adore the "Kilroy was here" from The Invasion, and I suspect that anyone who's heard at least one Hines/Troughton story has heard the one with Wendy Padbury's skirt "malfunction").

I've had the pleasure of meeting Frazer Hines at several conventions, most notably at Regenerations 2011 in Wales, which also featured all the surviving Second Doctor companions as guests. There, a bit of my Tumblr participation came full-circle. Since I'd already had some of my art signed at a preview event, I offered to get something signed for one of my TPC friends who was also a Classic Who artist. It was an illustration of Two and Jamie trying to blend in with a few other monsters on their way to Monty Python's Ministry of Silly Walks. My heart swelled quite a bit when Frazer saw it and said, "oh, she's very good!" But then it swelled even more when the guests were gathering for the group photo later that evening and Frazer walked in with Wendy on his arm. I saw them all together on a panel the next morning: Frazer, Wendy, Deborah, and Anneke, and I smiled and thought to myself "yes, still a family after all this time."

CHARACTER RETROSPECTIVE:
THE SECOND DOCTOR

I talked a bit in my last book about how much William Hartnell and the First Doctor helped shape both the show and the character, but I also feel that equal credit is due to Patrick Troughton. I think enough has been said already by everyone that the future of the show in 1966 depended entirely on how well he could carry the role, nothing like this had ever been done on television before, etc. But I think it bears repeating anyway: Hartnell started Doctor Who, but Troughton saved it. He proved that regeneration could work, and work well. He got audiences to keep watching, even forty-four years later when I first delved into the old serials. It was watching Two, Jamie, and Zoe in "The Mind Robber" late one night and deciding that I absolutely needed to finish all five episodes *right now* that I fell in love with Classic Who.

The Second Doctor is someone you really want to travel the universe with. He's warm and jolly, but also deceptively competent and rarely afraid to let his enemies underestimate him. Two is a bit like an inversion of One. Where Hartnell's Doctor was primarily authoritative with his kindliness showing through when needed, Troughton's is good-natured in his default state, but put his foot down when push came to shove. While Two doesn't undergo a proper character development arc, we do start to see some more of the Doctor's signature traits grow from him. He's the one who makes fighting evil and protecting the innocent his mission statement. While One certainly fought adversity where he found it, Two is the one who declared that it was his duty and responsibility as a space-time traveler. If the rest of the Time Lords refused to do right by their gifts, then he would do it himself. The Doctor was moving on to become more than the enigmatic leader of the TARDIS crew: he was becoming the Hero.

It's still a real shame that so much of this crucial period is still missing. The existence of reconstructions of the lost Troughton episodes are certainly a marvel in their own right, the purity of dedication that the fans have to recreating something out of almost nothing, but the operative word is still "lost." I think easily the biggest loss is how much less we get to see of Troughton's acting, because I think the sheer exuberance and charisma with which he fills the character is one of the Second Doctor's strongest suits. Two is just so much fun to *watch*. I want to see more of his wacky running. I want to see more of the faces he pulls at Jamie. But that's not to say I'm not still grateful for what we do have. The stories are still there to experience, even if we can't properly watch them. We can still read, we can still listen. The character of the Second Doctor still shines through the audio as a noble, bumbling, and entirely loveable Cosmic Hobo.

THE ENEMY OF THE WORLD: SPECIAL "OH MY GOD THEY FOUND THE THING" EDITION

Written by David Whitaker
Aired: December 23, 1967 – January 27, 1968

Yikes, the TARDIS doesn't sound well today...

Things I can SEE NOW OH MY GOD. I don't know what made me grin harder: Two's face, or Jamie's delightfully dorky sweater vest.

everything is patrick troughton dancing on the beach and nothing hurts

I love how Jamie and Victoria rapidly alternate from scoffing and sounding simply APPALLED that the Doctor would ask them to have FUN.

OH NO SANDCASTLES. THE VERY *THOUGHT*.

Meanwhile: a hovercraft. One of them seems to be sporting almost pre-Delgado facial hair.

I can't be the only one who saw that image of Two throwing his clothes off and jumping into the sea and thought "this is all I need in life"

Jamie your face is adorable but that laugh sounded almost demonic.

"Australasian Zone"? Hang on...hi Astrid!

Also, I can't get over how Anton holds exactly the same face for that entire conversation. #srysface

Actually, scratch that: this guy is Grumpy Cat with a gun.

Well, good thing you enjoyed your swim, Two, because now you've got would-be assassins coming after you in a sec.

"I'm too old for fairy tales!" Jamie...Jamie it's just a hovercraft...Jamie pls...

JAMIE AND VICTORIA ARE WEARING MATCHING KILTS. #jamieandvictoriaarewearingmatchingkilts

oh my god their running is so adorable and hilarious but the music is freakiNG TERRIFYING

I love how Two basically brushes the whole thing off with "oh don't worry, it's just humans who want to kill us."

Also can we talk about how Jamie shields the other two AND starts cracking his knuckles at Anton like "imma punch the SHIT outta you."

He's trying to be fierce but instead it's just adorable oh my god Jamie

HE ACTUALLY DID THE BATTLE CRY AND PUNCHED OUT AND VICTORIA'S CHEERING HIM THIS IS THE CUTEST FIGHT SCENE

Oh, so the guy Jamie punched wasn't Anton. Oh well...punching.

is this...yes...YES AFTER ALL THIS TIME WE FINALLY GET TO SEE THE HELICOPTER SCENE

Oh wow...with that pull-out shot, it looks like they *were* filming on an actual helicopter.

Although the cockpit has to be a studio shot. Hmm..."Valid Until 31st, Dec, 2018." Still got a good five more years on that thing.

can we talk about how Jamie has to move Victoria's arm off his face so he can ask a question #mostadorable

"They've shot a hole in the fuel tank. We might blow up any minute." OH. WELL THAT'S GOOD TO KNOW.

Ahh, safe landing. Wait...wasn't there something in the recon about them going upside-down a few times?

checks old commentary Huh. Maybe that comes later.

"It's nothing, it's just a scratch." Astrid...Astrid your hand is covered in blood.

"Doctor of...law? Philosophy?"
"Which law? Whose philosophies, eh?"

"Do you hate me?"
"Far from it. To me you're the most wonderful and marvelous man that's ever dropped out of the skies!"
#PAT #YOURFACE

guys guys guys he says he'll do anything with this big dopey grin and she says it may cost him his life and hIS FACE JUST DROOPS INSTANTLY

There are so many people to whom I just want to give an award to their face. Like...their face deserves an award.

How am I only just realizing that Astrid's coat is frickin fabulous.

Oh right...this episode's been gone for a while.

Umm...Astrid...are you sure they can't see you behind that sofa? That...kinda small sofa that you're not completely hidden behind?

Okay THIS must be the helicopter acrobatics scene I was thinking about before!

197

OH WAIT NO THIS IS THE OTHER THING

Here's a phrase I haven't used here in a while: and then there was a s'plosion!

"United Zones"...which is clearly the United Nations building, but okay.

Reeeeeaally not sure what to do with that accent, Pat.

So...the iTunes subtitles say "in our midst" when I'm pretty certain it's "in orbit." Because...it's the future...and it's a sun-catcher.

Jesus. I've never seen a man look and sound so menacing while talking about a successful crop.

"Remarkably handsome, didn't you think so, Jamie?" #yesdoctor #yesheis

Two...you'll forgive me for saying so, but I don't think turning a world dictator in to the police is as easy a feat as you think it is.

Face Award: Patrick Troughton trying to sound out phonetic differences in accent between two characters, one trying to sound like the other.

On that note, good luck compressing 3-4 weeks of accent mastery into as many minutes, because that's how long you have left in the episode.

Umm...I know this guy is supposed to be the security chief but...does he need to carry a riding crop around with him everywhere?

Okay so that's not a riding crop, but the way he said "I like to hear you say [who I am]" has a rather strong dom vibe about it.

"Whatarya doin here, ah?" Now that I can actually see it, this part walks a very fine line between tense and hilarious.

"Directed by Barry Letts." Huh, I didn't know he was a director for Troughton. I've always known him as Pertwee's producer.

I remember when I watched this for the recon, I made special note of Troughton's acting in this scene.

And now that I can SEE it, I can love it all the more. You can actually watch his face working to plot out what Two would say as Salamander.

With all that said...wow I'm still distracted by Jamie's outfit. It is at once both perfect and a fashion crime. How.

"I never said a word!"
"It must be the way you look, Jamie."
Speaking of which...

Actually, I just thought: has anyone ever made a complete timeline of Earth's alleged future according to Doctor Who?

Considering all the Classic stories that took place between then and "now," I imagine that would be...quite a feat, to say the least.

"Kanowa Research Station: Entry Forbidden Except With Planetary Pass" ...Planetary pass?

BENIIIIIKKKKK *hisses menacingly*

wait I'm already hating him a lot less and I can't explain why what is going on

Actually, it might just be watching Bruce be a bigger dick by comparison. The operative word may or may not be "watching."

Our first proper view of Salamander in person and he's all "volcanoes...guys I love volcanoes. Volcanoes are the *shit*. ...Volcanoes. :D"

"Volcanoes" doesn't even look like a real word anymore.

FARIAH! So great to see you again!

Jamie and Victoria on a Bench: with Special Guest Appearance by Jamie's Wristwatch.

"She's having spot trouble." ...There's a great euphemism in here somewhere, but I just can't pick one.

"My goodness, they're a pretty odd lot, aren't they?" I love how Two looks offended that someone would call his companions an "odd lot."

DISUSED JETTY/DISUSED YETI

Can we talk about that fact that even though Fariah is a servant alone with an official, she's clearly the one in power in this scene?

Because she is and I love it.

and look at how hard she's smiling when this guy thinks he's been poisoned oh my god #thebest

Suddenly, ACTION-JAMIE!

and he juST HOLDS OUT HIS ARMS IN A SHRUG LIKE "WELP I GUESS I JUST SAVED YOUR LIFE COOL STORY BRO" AND JAMIE I

HE'S LITERALLY JUST STANDING THERE WITH HIS ARMS FOLDED LIKE A BOSS EVEN THOUGH HE'S SURROUNDED BY GUNS #bestscot #battlekilt

Also, can we talk about the fact that Jamie isn't stumbling over future-isms in this scene like he usually does? #acting

"Yer security system's ROTTEN!" omg jamie pls

On a side-note, wow I wish getting a job these days was this easy.

Wow, that was the most beautifully over-dramatic music I've ever heard over a shot of someone sitting on a park bench and reading a book.

Last time I was wondering if they meant "girlfriend" romantically or "friend who is a girl..."

But...yeah, it seems pretty clear now that everyone thinks that Jamie and Victoria are dating.

Meanwhile at the yeti...erm, jetty...

"It was the safest place I could think of." ...Astrid that's literally just some wood and tall grass.

Like, could that guard walking past *seriously* not see you from the side? Because...it's almost insultingly easy to see you from the side.

Also, I'm no gun expert, but somehow I don't think holding the barrel that close to your face is such a good idea.

Fedorin mentions having a family, which tends to be fiction's minor character shorthand for "I'm going to die in this scene, aren't I?"

Purely for experiment's sake, I tried watching part of this scene with the sound off, just watching Troughton's face as Salamander.

It's a really fascinating blend of Two's facial tics but accented by a sinister demeanor and strategic use of Evil Eyebrows.

"Didn't I tell you? Denes is going to die. Mysteriously." Huh. So maybe I was wrong about that shorthand.

"My predictions are correct!" And that's Salamander's shorthand for "GUYS GUYYYYS LOOKIT THE VOLCANOES GUYYYYSSSS VOLCANOOOOES :D"

"The history of Hungary is about to be rewritten." Wait...where did this footage of streets being destroyed come from?

Oh hey Bruce yeah there was an attempt on my life no big deal COME AND LOOK AT MY VOLCANOOOOOEEEEEES. #basicallywhathesays

I find it odd and morbid that we have all this talk about Hungarians dying everywhere, and yet the destruction footage had NO people in it.

Right off the bat, Jamie in a leather suit.
#villainsandtheirfashionchoices

I love how Salamander keeps insisting that he's not blackmailing
Fedorin while conveniently falling in love with the word "insurance."

Also that he's reassuring Fedorin while wearing The Most Devious
Face and generally not looking reassuring at all.

Okay but seriously Bruce is like a full foot taller than Jamie and has
easily a hundred pounds on him and yet Jamie remains a steadfast
BAMF

"Why is Mr. Denses being kept in the corridor here?"
"It's easier to guard him here."
...How?

Can we talk about how Victoria's face just lights right up when she
talks about the pudding from home? #aww

Wait, Jamie, no, I know you want to show off your nice shiny new
suit to Victoria, but she and Fariah are busy having Srys Talk.

"Remove the honest man and put a weaker man in his place, but
somehow have a hold on him. That way Salamander will take over the
territory."

Really, though, I will probably fight anyone who calls Jamie "simple"
or "dumb."

"SECURITY, QUICK!" That actually sounds a bit more like an
ambulance..?

Boy, it's a good thing this Troughton-sized box just happens to be
right behind us!

(To be fair, I imagine Kent would have a lot of use for hidden spaces.
But I'm surprised he wasn't using that one for storage already.)

S'up Benik. Also, Kent, that was probably the most firm "look at
meeee, I'm not touching the liiiiiiine" variant I've heard in a while.

"It was just an accident." Ahhhhhhh yes, now I'm remembering why Benik is the biggest asshole in this story.

"After all, nobody would believe you, would they?" ...I seriously nearly just put my fist through my computer.

"Sad, really, isn't it? People spend all their time making nice things and then other people come along and break them."

One of my followers last time aptly replied to that line with "like Doctor Who episodes." Well, this one isn't broken anymore :)

Ah yes, the Brief Episode of Astrid Ferrier and Her Jacket Zipper.

I forgot how great Griff the Chef is. He's the closest we get to a Power Janitor in this story.

"Sometimes we do what we have to do, NOT what we want to do!" Okay seriously, David Whitaker HAD to've had a backstory in mind for Fariah.

The way she talks implies a specific chain of events and morals that led her to where she is now, but we never actually learn what that was.

Adventures in Getting Really Invested in the Supporting Cast: The Blog

"Who's gonna control this zone now? Fedorin?"
SEMI-DRAMATIC CLOSE-UP "Fedorin...oh what a good idea!"

Did...did Victoria seriously not see him take the salt?

Ah, THERE'S our dramatic musical cue!

"And how do you cut a steak with a spoon?" It's not that hard, actually. I've done it before. Or was that with chicken...

Huh. I was wondering why the dramatic cue over the salt was slightly muted. Fedorin lost his nerve in the end. Good man.

Salamander's taking this surprisingly well oh wait he's going to poison Fedorin instead never mind

"I have an alternative." *hands over poison glass* "Your health."
#Iseewhatyoudidthere

"It's made for me specially in Alaska." ...can you even grow wine
grapes in Alaska

Hey guard can you take care of this dead body on my balcony kthanx
#salamanderproblems

ACTION ACTION ESCAPE SHOVE THE FOOD CART *JUMP
CUT* wait a minute how did we get to Salamander's office all of a
sudden.

"It was you! Or...someone like you..." I love how hard this show can
imply a DUN DUN DUUUUUN without actually using one.

How have I gone this long without mentioning that Two standing
around looking sheepish and fiddling with his fingers is Super
Adorable?

Ceiling Benik is watching you communicate.

I'm really proud of Doctor Who for having two women engaging in
a struggle without making it look like a catfight.

On that note... "I want to be there to see his face when he DIES!"
...daily reminder that Fariah is amazeballs.

Oh Benik, your ears are just so damn boxable. Also, you really seem
to enjoy rolling Fariah's name around in your mouth.

We're four episodes in and Two *still* somehow doesn't have his
proof that Salamander is a bag of dicks? Really?

Maybe I've been out of the Two loop for too long, but I don't
remember him being this reluctant to help and having such little
confidence.

On the other hand none of his other stories have him dealing with
someone else played by Patrick Troughton, so...yeah, that would be
tricky.

Aaaaand now he's got Kent to admit that he wants Two to kill Salamander. Now his insistent No's make much more sense.

Also I feel like I could watch this scene over and over again just for the sake of watching more of Troughton's face moving.

A directoral appreciation: every shot back and forth between Two and Kent zooms in tighter on their faces and ups the tension like woah.

The other upside of this is, of course, that we get more close-ups of Patrick Troughton's magnificent face.

Taking a break from glaring at Benik's slimeball face to notice that the stone background is, in fact, wallpaper and not real stone.

Woah, hold on, this is the first exterior shot we've had of Kent's place...and it's in a apartment building?

I'd always thought it was just a house in the middle of nowhere, but I guess that was Astrid's place. This has, like, balconies and stuff.

Astrid Ferrier: Always and Forever a BAMF woah wait a second who's that rappeling in through the window like a goddamn ninja

"He's outside the window now, sir." Oh, just another guard.

Oh come on, Astrid, you had such a clear shot to kick that guy in the nuts. If the Rani can do it, so can you.

(Actually I imagine there's quite a few things the Rani can do that Astrid can't, but that's a discussion for another day.)

Benik for christsake the woman's already dying DON'T HOLD A GUN TO HER STOMACH AND DEMAND INTEL FROM HER THAT'S JUST MESSED UP

"You can't threaten me now, Benik. I can only die once...and someone's beaten you to it." #famouslastwords

SHE FUCKIN SLAPPED HIM SECONDS BEFORE SHE DIED

OH MY GOD REST IN AWESOME FARIAH YOU WERE THE BEST

And yet Benik still manages to walk off with "I'll take that last laugh, thank you very much."

I have a weird appreciation for the fact that he took the time to fix his hair before going to see Salamander and Bruce.

...And for his usual sinister grin turning into a schoolboy grin when he hands Salamander the file and is like look sir I found the thing :D

Hang on...ah, THIS must be that weird transportation scene from the recon that I really couldn't comprehend without footage.

Huh. All he did was get into an elevator chute-thing and seemed mildly okay with zooming down at drop-tower speeds. Okay.

Also, I kinda wanted that little scene of Bruce and Benik trying to outrank each other to go on a little longer.

Meanwhile underground, Salamander's ditched his Mexican garb and...are those people wearing doctor's-office-wallpaper gowns?

Ah yes, the sudden introduction of the subterranean scientists/ rebels/volcanomancers.

"We have to fight for a while longer, creating natural disasters, monsoons, earthquakes, volcanic eruptions..." okay but HOW.

I mean I understood the first time that they were making that happen, just now...how that was physically possible.

Also it seems that everyone down below knows what they're doing, just under the pretense of a nuclear war on the surface.

"I'd rather die with you up on the surface than live down here without you." #see #seetheyreinlove #didyouseethat #seewhatwedidthere

I kinda love how we transition from Salamander chilling underground with a cigar to Two indignantly suffering through a haircut.

Interesting. In previous episodes Troughton was credited as "Dr.
Who Salamander," but now they're finally pulling a slash between the
names.

Aww, seeing Two get caught in full Salamander get-up is kinda like
watching a kid get caught with his hand in the cookie jar.

Oh god, and the hands clasped over the mouth after he accidentally
outed Fariah made it even better.

"I do things my own way."
steals giant gun "And I do things MY way!"
ASTRID I LOVE YOU

Bruce has the best face right now. It's a perfect mix of "well, I'm
impressed" and "welp, I done goofed."

Jamie and Victoria just got carried by on stretchers THAT'S NOT
AN ALARMING IMAGE AT ALL (seriously they look dead).

"I'm looking forward to questioning them. I have a feeling they're
going to be stubborn." Benik there are children watching.

Um, Two, I'm pretty sure following up "I will not have anything to
do with violence!" with asking to borrow someone's gun is...not a
thing.

Well, at least he has the courtesy to say "please, just trust me."

"I gave you back that gun because I trust you." TWO WHAT ARE
YOU EVEN DOING

"And what do you hope to gain by this gesture?"
"Your confidence."
oh my god I think this plan is actually working

"Milk: Glass" Would they really be keeping milk in glass bottles
during wartime, though? War tends to break glass.

...I just realized I was implying that plastic or cardboard cartons were
somehow war-proof. #whoops

I find it kind of hilarious that Colin has virtually no character beyond "SURFACE NOW PLEASE."

"Meat: Fragile" OKAY HOW IS MEAT FRAGILE. IT'S *MEAT*.

Hang on, looks like Swann found a stray newspaper clipping on the underside of the fragile meat box. #everythingyouknowisalie

"HOW can there be holiday liners? HOW? ...You've lied to us, haven't you?" Aaaand there's Salamander's hand in the volcanic cookie jar.

Salamander seems to be trying to worm his way out of this by reinforcing exactly what he was telling them before. Because that always works.

Actually, it's more like TRUST ME I'VE SEEN THE THING. HAVE YOU SEEN THE THING? OF COURSE NOT YOU SHOULD LISTEN TO ME I'VE SEEN THE THING

"I won't take your word anymore." #youneversawthething

"Very well...but promise me one thing: you won't tell the others." Salamander's just gonna kill Swann on the surface, isn't he?

"And if you're lying and I WANT to tell them when I get back?" "How can I stop you?" careful swann that means he's gonna kill you

Oh no, Swann looks like he's about to cry D:

"He's going to take me with him!" ... "But why not me? Why? I asked him. He turned me down! Why not me? WHY NOT ME??" Colin #we #get #it

Jamie and Victoria are finally up! Well that only took half the episode.

"Don't leave us so soon. We can have a little talk." benik no

Incidentally, did they really have the door unlocked that whole time?

"Come now, you don't think I'm just going to sit here and ask questions, do you?" BENIK NO

in the span of five seconds we have jamie punching a dude and benik getting victoria at gunpoint how did they even

"Oh, we're going to enjoy ourselves, aren't we?" B E N I K N O

I'm literally flailing around in my seat this scene is super-uncomfortable but why am I enjoying it

I JUST REALIZED I DON'T THINK BENIK HAS BLINKED THIS ENTIRE SCENE

Okay, I was wrong. But he does seem to go eerily long periods without blinking.

Twomander! What perfect timing! #whew

Troughton's acting, though. You can HEAR little bits of Two coming through in those tiny pauses when he isn't sure what to say mid-sentence.

OH MY GOD AND HE KEEPS THE ACT GOING PERFECTLY UNTIL VICTORIA RUSHES OVER TO *SMACK HIM*

NOW HE'S PLAYING TWINKLE TWINKLE LITTLE STAR WHILE FIRMLY IGNORING THAT HE DOESN'T EVEN HAVE HIS RECORDER PAT HOW ARE YOU REAL

also can we talk about the fact that Jamie is reaching all the way around Victoria to clutch at Two's shoulder because

Is it just me, or does Kent lose most of his accent when he lowers his voice?

"Oh, we're not going to attack the guard, but there IS going to be an attack. A fatal one!" ...astrid your face what are you planning

Salamader, you seem to be past the point of subtlety. Do you really think Swann doesn't see you picking up that pipe on the crate?

*insert I am a Trained Soldier Who Cannot Tell the Difference

Between Blood and Ketchup joke here* (apologies to hiimdaisy)

Astrid, I'll be frank: I'm AMAZED that that plan worked.

That cry for help sounds like it's coming from...underground? Oh no, Swann...

Oh wait, he was aboveground. And Astrid, why do you look surprised by Salamander's dickery at this point?

It's okay, Bruce, we're just as confused about how refugees in an underground lab can create natural disasters as you are.

Although, if the earthquakes and volcanoes are actually man-made... then they technically aren't *natural* disasters, are they?

S'up Benik.

Well, at least Astrid's tasting the cave-wall water before she gives it to Swann.

"*whew* That was close!" NO TWO DON'T YOU SEE BENIK'S ON TO YOU.

"D'you think he's onto us?"
"...I hope not."
#heis

Looks like Astrid didn't have enough water to actually *give* to Swann, so she just wet a hankie to cool him off with.

Which, I must say, sounds preferable to the recon version where (if I remember right) she straight up gives him cave-wall water.

They cut straight from Astrid comforting a dying Swann to Twomander on the phone, and for some reason I burst out laughing.

"Tell him where I am and just say 'redhead'."
"'Redhead'."
"'Redhead.' Is that clear?"
"'Redhead'...is that yer wife?"
jamie pls

I love how Two doesn't even get to finish his sentence of "you two go straight back to the TARDIS" before they start protesting.

Astrid has arrived below! Maybe now we can get things straightened out with the poor prisoners.

A mysterious woman has come down from the surface and says she wants to help us! WE MUST BEAT HER WITH STICKS.

Astrid Ferrier is 2017% done.

...Okay, now I'm honestly not sure if that's Salamander or Twomander fiddling with that machine.

I really do admire Astrid's commitment to being as firm and dramatic with everything she says. #forEMPHASIS

Benik...Benik did you seriously not see Kent hiding just around that corner...Benik...okay...

Okay now I REALLY have no idea if that's Salamander or Twomander confronting Kent.

ACTUALLY WAIT. I bet that IS Twomander, since Kent left the monitor on outside so Benik could see them and try to break the door down.

I WAS RIGHT IT *WAS* TWOMANDER.

...oh my god Two was setting Kent up the whole time.

So...where exactly is Salamander watching THEM from? Still in the tunnels?

"Any man who resorts to murder as eagerly and as rapidly as you MUST be suspect. You didn't just want to expose Salamander, you wanted to kill him and take his place!"
"AND I WILL!!!"

Wait...what exactly prompted Benik to make a break for it and suddenly reveal himself for the cowardly weasel he really is?

"I think Kent is going to try and blow us up! Any chance of getting us out of here? Things are going to turn rather nasty in a minute!"

Now that we have the full episode I can finally appreciate the LIGHTING in this scene. Salamander vs. Kent. Final Round.

Impressive that Kent made it out with just a small bloom of blood and no bullet hole in his shirt...

Aaaaaand boom goes the dynamite. #thentherewasasplosion Also, perfect timing on that door, Bruce!

...Wow. Jamie and Victoria actually DID go straight back to the TARDIS. Except...uh oh...Jamie that's not Two...

The one fault of having the visuals again: there's little mystery left in this last scene of who's who.

You can tell it's Salamander because he's not responding to Jamie and he's looking at the TARDIS console like "buttons...how do..."

"You're doing so well impersonating me, well, I thought I might return the compliment."

YESSSSS. YES IT'S THE FIGHT SCENE WE DIDN'T GET TO SEE BEFORE.

And Salamander gets thrown out into the time vortex. What a way to die.

So this episode ran two minutes short, and I feel like there was one more scene with Astrid missing...

Oh. Guess not. For some reason I was remembering her dying. Probably thinking of Swann's death.

THE MIND ROBBER:
REVISITED AND EXTENDED COMMENTARY

Written by Peter Ling and Derrick Sherwin
Aired: September 14 – October 12, 1968

Meanwhile at the end of The Dominators...Two...Two there's a volcano erupting...Two...

Huh, looks like Zoe's caught the Salamander bug of "GUYS GUYS VOLCANOOOOOES VOLCANOES GUYS."

"The fluid links don't seem to be able to take the load..." GODDAMN FLUID LINKS

"Oh, don't worry, Jamie, we're safe in the TARDIS." Sure, you'll probably suffocate from mercury inhalation, but it's better than lava.

(Seriously, though, that does sound like a preferable way of dying to getting burned alive.)

In case of emergency, please cling to your nearest Doctor.

"There y'are, we're alright. What was all the panic about?" Well... getting removed from reality sounded like something to panic about.

Jamie sure is taking this whole we're-literally-nowhere pretty well, isn't he?

Ah yes, the debut of the Sparkly Catsuit.

I don't think we've had any music yet, but I don't think we need any? Because the TARDIS humming honestly makes a perfect ambiance.

And of course literally RIGHT after I type that...bagpipes.

oh my god it's just jamie staring at scotland with bagpipes in the background and it's so adorable but I caN'T STOP LAUGHING

LIKE I'M PRETTY SURE THIS ONE SHOT IS AS SCOTTISH AS THE ENTIRE THE HIGHLANDERS SERIAL. IT IS PURE CONCENTRATED SCOT.

"Scotland?"
"Aye! ...oh...well it WAS there..."
:(

"It's the city...my home!" Ah yes, Nonspecific Futuristic Sci-Fi-Tropolis as Imagined by 1968.

That reminds me, we never find out exactly where Zoe's from, do we? Just 21st Century Earth?

What's that, Doctor? Zoe's run out into an unidentifiable white mist outside reality? Action Scot to the rescue!

Two will not be swayed by your warning alarms. DEFIANCE CHAIR!

Meanwhile in Nothing...

hand-holding awwwww

Jamie come on, this is no time to be feeling yourself up.

Umm, Two, hate to break it to you, but...that desperate yelling IS actually your companions crying out for help.

Incoming White Robots!

"It's almost as thought I was seeing what I most wanted to see..."

Oh...OH GOD

GUYS ALL OF TIME AND SPACE BUT WHAT THEY MOST
WANTED TO SEE WAS HOME. THIS STORY JUST BECAME
WAY TOO SAD.

ALSO ZOE JUST SMACKED JAMIE (okay, I guess friends
in fiction are allowed to hit friends if they need an Emergency
Hallucination Solution.)

In case of emergency, please cling to your nearest Zoe.

I apologize in advance for this morbidly obvious joke, but...come play
with us, Doctor...for ever and ever...

Also, I don't know why people say that Mel is the biggest screamer in
Doctor Who when Zoe's is shriller by a long shot.

Wow, even the TARDIS turned white.

Back inside, ready for something else to go wrong any second now...

Wait, we're only 17 minutes into the episode. How does...ohhhhh
right, this was that one where all the episodes were shorter...or most.

Jamie how did you even fall asleep that fast. "Quiet, Jamie!" Yes, this
is no time for having nightmares about unicorns, young man!

Also it feels weird hearing you say "what's up." I didn't think that was
an 18th century colloquialism.

This scene is becoming an excellent gallery of Patrick Troughton's
Amazing Face.

TARDIS-SPLOSION

Aaaaand there goes the infamous glitterbum.

Hold up, if Jamie and Zoe were on the console together just a second
ago, how did they get separated? Unless they crashed or something.

"Shoot me down like a dog, would ye?" Jamie McCrimmon: literally bringing a knife to a gun fight.

Aaaaand off goes poor Frazer with the chicken pox.

"JAMIE! DOCTOR! HELP! SOMEBODY HELP ME, I'M TRAPPED!" Oh hello, Creakiest Door in the Universe. Care to let Zoe out? Thanks, you're a dear.

And then you go and drop her down a pit? Now that wasn't very considerate of you, door.

Ah yes, our Man Hidden in the Shadows of the hour.

"NO NO NO NO NO!!! NOT BOTH TOGETHER, ONE AT A TIME! Now then...Jamie you seem to be the nearer, you first." #priorities

"This is like exploring a maze in the dark." And lo, there was light. And Two saw it, and Two saw that it was good.

Yikes, I hate to think how hard it was for those poor actors in the toy soldier suits to move around.

What...is that even a real language...Two what makes you think that's French...

The InfoText is listing it as Lilliputian and...Brobdingnagian? And Firefox is recognizing both as real words?

looks it up Aaaaaha. Further proof to my dear followers that I have not, in fact, read Gulliver's Travels. Yet.

"What became of my companions I cannot tell. They were all lost."
"Oh my dear sir! You and I are in the same boat!"
"You have a stout ship?"

Our first mention of Master-not-Master!

Ah. Hello sudden Small Army of Creepy Children.

"HURRAY!!!" *sword becomes dictionary* #wellokaythen

Apparently if you throw a dictionary down a wishing well, a disembodied voice will laugh at you.

"Jamie is...safe and well! ...Oh no I've lost his face!" Now there's two sentences you don't want to hear in that order.

Actually I'm pretty sure the second one is a sentence you don't want to hear ever.

("The script calls for Patrick Troughton to ad-lib his dialogue as he reassembles Jamie's face.") Aww, so the nose thing was his idea!

Seriously though, the "that's his nose alright!" is one of the most adorable things in this whole story.

On that note, hello Hamish!

"What's the good of thinking? What we need's a BATTERING RAM." omg jamie pls

Ahahahahah, yes, let's all have a good laugh at Zoe trapped in a jar before letting her out :)

"It's a forest of words!" My inner English major is grinning like a loon.

"We hide, in among the trees! There's a J, there's room for two! Oh thank goodness, there's a letter C!"

Welp, there's your Nightmare Unicorn, Jamie.

"IT'S COMING STRAIGHT FOR US!" #alwaysIwannabewithyou #andmakebelievewithyou #andliveinharmonyharmonyOHLOVE

Ah, saved by the power of unbelieving! Funny, usually it's the other way around.

Wait, is the Master holding a knife? What does he even have to stab?

Welcome back, Frazer! Speaking of stabbing, I'm not sure you should be holding your dirk that close to your face.

Whoops. This doesn't look like the best time to be running out of string.

...Yikes, where'd that skeleton come from?

"Ah, so that's how you can see, is it? That wee lighthouse of yours." Wee lighthouse. #weelighthouse

Apparently the one shot of the minotaur head was BBC stock footage. Still somehow better-looking than the Nimon.

"This world that we've tumbled into is a world of fiction!" I will never not love just how meta this story is.

Huh, apparently the tin solder chasing Jamie up a cliff was Frazer Hines' cousin. #themoreyouknow

Also, wow, Jamie's scaling those rocks with remarkable speed. Doubly impressive because apparently this was on location...?

Huh, I didn't even know there was any location filming for this story. Seems like it would be pretty studio-bound.

Although watching a giant tin soldier chasing a Scotsman up a cliff must've been an interesting sight for onlookers.

"What I really need is a..." *convenient rope* "...who says wishes don't come true?"

And now we're back in the studio. Hello Rapunzel!

"You're not a woodcutter's son, by any chance?"
"Erm, no, I'm the son of a piper!"
"Oh, how very disappointing."

I kinda love how the InfoText is actually retelling the whole Rapunzel story. I honestly don't know who would've grown up NOT knowing it.

A mysterious room full of futuristic tech inside a castle? Better turn some random knobs and see what happens.

Wow, that's probably the biggest e-reader screen I've ever seen.

Oh no, it's fanfiction! On ticker tape!

"That wasn't there before."
"A statue."
NO GUYS THAT'S THE MEDUSA GET OUT OF THERE

Ack, from this angle it kinda looks like Zoe's hair is on fire. #unfortunatelyplacedcandles

("In the script Medusa takes Zoe's face and turns it, forcing the girl to look at her.") JESUS CHRIST THAT WOULD'VE BEEN A GREAT CLIFFHANGER

Although I have a sneaking suspicion they changed it because that version would've been a bit much.

Only just noticing that the Ticker Tape Fanfiction Dome has a "work in progress" sticker on it.

SUDDENLY, A SWORD!

"How can I kill something that doesn't exist?" TWO, FOR ONCE THIS REALLY MIGHT BE A GREAT TIME TO START STABBING THINGS.

Or you could use a mirror, that works too.

Jamie how...how did you open up the wall like that...

You know, I bet Gulliver can't see the robots because his book doesn't contain the word "robot," so he can't know what they are.

Aww, poor Jamie looks so done.

"You will come out and put ze hands above ze head!" Hello Karkus!

219

Action-Zoe vs. Karkus: Round 1. FIGHT!

oh my god while kicking his ass Zoe LITERALLY KICKED HIM IN THE ASS

Strip cartoons? Well yeah, that guy was practically half-naked...oh, wait, THOSE kinds of strips.

can we talk about how all zoe needs to do is snap her fingers and karkus just goes "I obey" oh my god how can you not love this girl

"We can't just ring the bell and ask to go in!"
"Why not? It's the usual way."

Our trio reunited! Now to figure out how to get past the electronic tripwire.

Ah, that was easy. And Jamie has his Reversible Cow Vest back!

"Yer not really going to do as he says, are you?"
"No, of course not. I said I'd think it over, well I've thought it over!"

And now it's time to play How Meta Can We Get?
"If we'd fallen into the Master's trap, we would have BECOME fiction!"
"Oh that's horrible!"

Incoming White Robots! Quick, initiate the Cling Train!

"Zoe and Jamie, I have your dossiers here in front of me!"
#canIputmydossieronthetable

"Another power, higher than you could begin to imagine!" I have to wonder if the Master is suggesting the existence of God here.

"Captain Jack Harkaway," the poor man's Captain Jack Harkness, I presume?

...Wait. According to the InfoText, Jack Harkaway WAS an actual magazine serial character from 1871. Wow.

"That means that you are...virtually a prisoner!"
"Oh, no! No no no!"
The ominous humming from the machine behind you begs to differ.

"I REFUSE!"
"REFUSAL. IS. IMPOSSIBLE!"
Well, that's inconvenient.

...I can't be the only one who froze a little when Jamie almost impaled himself on one of the White Robot's chest spikes just now.

The robots are trying to melt our brains! Quick, hide in this French book! WAIT NO THIS WAS A BAD PLAN NOPE

"WHAT HAVE YOU DONE TO THEM?"
"They're no longer human beings, just fictional characters!"
#THISLINETHOUGH

did two just rapidly ascend a sparsely-loaded bookshelf without it falling over

"They're not real, they've been turned into fiction..." no no no Two don't sad Two D:

Hey Karkus, think you could bust open that skylight for Two? He needs to write some fix-it fic.

Ah, thank you Rapunzel! Sorry, but your prince is in another castle.

can we stop and talk about the fact that this climax hinges on Two writing anything BUT self-insert fic because

"I understand, sir, that you are in an unhappy situation." Really, Gulliver? I never would've guessed. #poortwo

The TARDIS is back! And Jamie and Zoe are back to norm...wait. WAIT.

Evil!Jamie and evil!Zoe giggling and rubbing their hands together is way more adorable than it reasonably should be.

221

Although the children running up to laugh at Two in the box are exactly as creepy as they reasonably should be.

"Sausages! Man will just become like a string of sausages! All the same!" That...Two where exactly did that analogy come from.

Two vs. Master-not-Master: Round 2. FIGHT!

One of the cutest things about Jamie is when he clings to Zoe I'm never sure if he's being protective of her or just needs to hold somebody.

The fact that she's a good half-a-foot shorter than him makes it even better.

"And now, Doctor, OBEY ME!"
"NO!"
...Master-maybe-more-the-Master-than-we-thought

Guys I think this just turned into The Oldest Game.

AND THEN IT TURNED INTO A POKEMON BATTLE BETWEEN LITERARY HEROES. CYRANO, D'ARTAGNAN, I CHOOSE YOU!

Checked the InfoText to see what this music is and it's...a scherzo. Guys...don't make me have Eight-feels in the middle of a fun Two romp.

CYRANO, RETURN. BLACKBEARD, GO! D'ARTAGNAN, RETURN. LANCELOT, GO!

Aww, they almost had Zorro in there as well! That would've been so cool! But, copyright.

Press ALL the buttons!

"Zoe, let's get out of here and duck!" Yes, but in which order?

"Oh! Do you mean I'm going home?"

"Well I hope so!"
...considering we don't see him at all at the start of The Invasion, I don't know...

Although, I'll bet the assumption was that they'd be sent back to where they were right when they were taken into the Land of Fiction.

TARDIS is back for real this time and...the end! *sigh* As much as I love this serial, I'm still not fond of the abrupt ending.

About the Author

Hannah J. Rothman is an American Whovian who came to the party a little late. By the time she started watching *Doctor Who*, the 2009 specials were well underway and by the time she was officially a fan, the Tenth Doctor was pleading "I don't want to go." She spent the following year (particularly that summer) soaking up as much Classic Who as humanly possible, drawing fan art, contributing to the fanzine *The Terrible Zodin*, developing preposterous amounts of head-canon for the Fifth Doctor and his original trio of sadly underdeveloped companions, and making some wonderful friends in the fandom online. There was also a lot of Tweeting. Hannah sports a BA in English and currently lives in bustling New York City, where she has thankfully never encountered any Daleks on the Empire State Building. Her other geeky writing can be found in *Outside In*, the upcoming *Outside In 2* and *3*, and *Chicks Dig Gaming*.

Connect with Hannah Online:

Website: http://hannahjrothman.com

Twitter: https://twitter.com/WhoBlogLiveFeed

The original blog: http://classicwhoblog.livejournal.com/

FURTHER EXPLORATION

Want to watch the Tweets as they happen? Join me at
https://twitter.com/WhoBlogLiveFeed

Join the discussion! Visit the original blog archive at
http://classicwhoblog.livejournal.com/

**For pictures, photonovels, detailed episodes guides, and more,
visit the BBC's official Classic Who site at**
http://www.bbc.co.uk/doctorwho/classic/

**For even more photo fun, check out Doctor Who's Tragical
History Tour at**
http://tragicalhistorytour.com/

BY WHOVIANS FOR WHOVIANS, AUTHOR'S CHOICE FANWORKS:

Pick up the complete free catalogue of *The Terrible Zodin* **fanzine
at**
http://doctorwhottz.blogspot.com/

Listen in to the TARDIS Tavern podcast on iTunes or at
http://tardistavern.libsyn.com/

ALSO AVAILABLE

TWITTER WHO VOLUME 1:
THE FIRST DOCTOR

A JOURNEY OF 100 SERIALS BEGINS WITH A SINGLE TWEET.

Okay, more than 100.

Whofolk, you are hereby invited to the first chapter of an epic quest as one lone fan traverses the vast realm of Classic Who through fresh eyes: a fan born...wait for it...after 1989. The journey ahead is long and intricate and she wields one tool to document it: Twitter. Bursting from the pages of *Outside In*, Hannah J. Rothman returns to the beginning as she Tweets and commentates her way through the complete William Hartnell era of *Doctor Who*. Grab your lapels and get your sonics ready.

AVAILABLE IN PRINT AND ALL EBOOK FORMATS AT YOUR FAVORITE BOOKSTORES.

Made in the USA
San Bernardino, CA
13 May 2015